THE **WOODWORKER'S** STUDIO HANDBOOK

Brimming with creative inspiration, how-to projects, and useful information to enrich your everyday life, Quarto Knows is a favorite destination for those pursuing their interests and passions. Visit our site and dig deeper with our books into your area of interest: Quarto Creates, Quarto Cooks, Quarto Homes, Quarto Lives, Quarto Drives, Quarto Explores, Quarto Gifts, or Quarto Kids.

Project Design and Production: Jim Whitman
Book Design: Laure H. Couallier, Laura Herrmann Design
Photography: Randy O'Rourke, except where noted

10 9 8 7 6 5 4 3 2 1

ISBN: 978-0-7858-3723-7

Printed in China

THE WOODWORKER'S STUDIO HANDBOOK

Traditional and Contemporary Techniques for the Home Woodworking Shop

Jim Whitman

CRESTLINE

Contents

Introduction

The knowledge I've gained during thirty-five years of woodworking was brought to light when I started writing this book. The diary of woodworking skills that I had filed away in my brain were rigorously tested as I tried to extrapolate them to paper. To write about all these skills and experiences would be like writing *War and Peace*; I can only touch on a small portion of them in this slim, but comprehensive, volume.

Learning how to make "wood work" does not happen overnight. Reading about it and watching woodworkers on television or video will get your creative juices flowing, but it is the hands-on practice that truly hones your woodworking skills. The same is true of any discipline: An artist never learns to draw by watching someone else draw.

Most woodworking schools teach students how to work with hand tools before using machinery. These skills are the most rewarding because they teach you how to cut, shape, form, and smooth wood by hand. Working with hand tools teaches you how to read the grain, determining what direction to cut and how to prevent tear out. Measure twice, cut once. And further, making mistakes is a great teacher. The connection of hand and tool to caress the wood will give you a feeling of great satisfaction. You will whistle while you work!

It is no sin to use handheld power tools while honing your woodworking skills. It is counterproductive to use a hand screwdriver when an electric hand drill is sitting on the bench. Hand tools and handheld power tools make good partners.

It took me years to gather all the power and hand tools shown in this book. I started out in my basement with an old radial arm saw and an assortment of my father's hand-me-downs. This was a good way to start out. It taught me to work with what I had. I moved my family three times before we settled down on our farm. Each move allowed me a larger work space. I finally have my dream shop in the barn, but I still think I need more room!

In the following chapters, I give many suggestions about setting up your shop, introduce you to tools and techniques, and instruct how to build projects using several different woodworking disciplines. I then show you how to finish these projects beautifully. Some of the dimensions used in the plans for the projects in this book can be changed or altered to meet your specific needs, once you are fluent in your skills.

There are many ways to acquire more knowledge and improve your skills. A self-taught woodworker can, in time, become a successful artisan, most certainly. Attending woodworking classes and seminars opens more avenues for success. I have

> "There is no better feeling than when you present your latest creation to family or friends and they touch and feel it and exclaim, 'Wow, you made this?'"

been fortunate to be associated with Peters Valley Craft Center in northern New Jersey for the past thirty years. During this period I attended many workshops taught by world-renowned teachers such as Sam Maloof, Tage Frid, Mack Headley, Stephen Proctor, and Jere Osgood, to mention a few. These sessions were inspirational as well as educational.

The demise of teaching shop skills in our schools has left a couple of generations of youth without an introduction to the wood shop. Students are now encouraged to make robots and solar-powered cars to keep up with modern technology. Luckily, some school systems are now inviting craft centers to offer woodworking and craft demonstrations to show students basic skills and kindle their interest in classic crafts.

If your interest is piqued by this book, you will never be short on more sources of information and inspiration. There are many teaching craft centers around the world as well as woodworking clubs and guilds. Many well-known woodworkers conduct lessons in their own studios.

One of the most thrilling experiences in woodworking I've had was in the late 1970s when I visited the studio and compound of George Nakashima in New Hope, Pennsylvania. This was my introduction to the Japanese sensitivity of form and function and simplicity of design. His approach to turning a tree into a piece of functional art has inspired me for decades. These are the kind of inspirational experiences that everyone should look for, be it in a Shaker village or in the great museums of the world.

Don't forget your sketchbook and pencil as you travel down this road! It is important to sketch, draw, or even scribble your ideas. These can later be refined and adapted to create a plan for your next project or for future use.

As you progress and your skills come together, beautiful objects start to appear. There is no better feeling than when you present your latest creation to family or friends and they touch and feel it and exclaim, "Wow, you made this?"

—*Jim Whitman*

CHAPTER

1

Setting up
the Studio

Building furniture and accessories in your own workshop is a fulfilling experience. Having a comfortable area to work in will be reflected both in the quality of your craft and your safety.

Setting up your studio or woodworking shop can be a challenge, but an inspiring one. You must first decide what type of woodwork you intend to do, as that will determine what type of space and equipment you will need.

If you want to carve wood or turn on a lathe, less space is needed than if you want to build furniture. Starting small is a must for some people because space is simply not available. Small areas properly laid out can be all a creative woodworker needs to produce great work. No matter how big or small your space is, planning your layout, lighting, access, storage, utilities, and safety will make it a pleasure to work with wood.

Being able to hold your work firmly on your workbench assures accuracy, such as during hand planing (shown here).

Work Space

Making do with the space and resources you have is the first lesson everyone faces when starting out with any new hobby. Your space may be limited or you may have a large, well-lit room that is perfect for becoming a woodshop. As a new, enthusiastic woodworker, your mandate is to make the most of available resources while envisioning future growth.

Is your work space adequate for accommodating the type of woodworking you want to do? You may find that your basement is a good place to set up shop, as long as it doesn't interfere with the rest of the family. Many basement woodshops have enabled the craftsperson to produce beautiful work.

Other shops may share or take over garage space. Some studios are set up in outbuildings or barns as more space is needed. Proper planning is very important in designing your work area. Is there room for growth? Can you comply with local zoning restrictions?

Even if you live in an apartment, you can still find room for your woodworking hobby. You just need to be efficient and clever. A corner of a shared basement or garage, even a closet, can house a portable workbench. And if you are a wood carver, cleanup will always be simple as you will only create wood chips, not dust.

If space is at a premium, there are many other clever measures you can take:

- Arrange large equipment, such as a planer or table saw, in front of an open door or doorway. This allows you to rip or plane long boards by passing them through the opening.

- Create storage for hand power tools, such as routers, drills, sanding equipment, and more, under existing benches.

- Find new storage solutions. There are underutilized areas in your living space that are perfect for cabinets and shelving. Maximizing your space will make your tools quickly accessible when needed but off the bench when not in use.

If you live in a region where weather is mild most of the year, you can set up a workbench outdoors or under a covered area. Working outside is ideal when you are sanding or doing finishing work, when ventilation is mandatory. Many woodworking tasks can be done outside as weather permits.

ELECTRICITY

Aside from space, another major factor to consider when planning your work area is having access to adequate electricity. Electricity runs your machinery and provides good, abundant lighting, and it should be equally well planned in shops built into basements, garages, or separate buildings. Adequate electric outlets minimize the need for extension cords lying across your shop floor.

If you are planning to install additional electrical lines to outfit your work space:

- Always have a licensed electrician install or upgrade your electric service.

- Electrical outlets should be placed every 8' for 110-V service. Place the outlets 36" or more off the floor. This lets you plug in your equipment without stooping down to baseboard level and keeps the outlets above bench height.

- Ideally, 220-V service should extend from cords suspended from the ceiling over the appropriate machines. This will allow you to plug in your heavy equipment safely without having cords draped across the floor.

- Separate circuit breakers should divide 220-V and 120-V service. Running three machines that require 220-V service with the balance of the equipment on 110-V, a minimum of 100-amp service should be considered. Remember that no two machines will be running at the same time in a one-person shop (except for the dust collector).

- Most 220-V machinery, such as jointers, planers, and table saws, requires 20- to 30-amp service. Equipment that runs on 120-V usually needs 15-amp service. Always refer to your user manual for the proper electrical requirements.

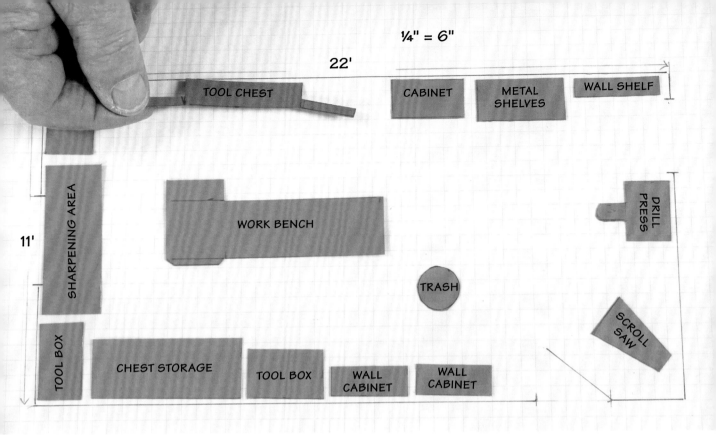

¼" = 6'

22'

11'

TOOL CHEST

CABINET

METAL SHELVES

WALL SHELF

SHARPENING AREA

WORK BENCH

DRILL PRESS

TRASH

TOOL BOX

CHEST STORAGE

TOOL BOX

WALL CABINET

WALL CABINET

SCROLL SAW

Laying out your studio in a two-dimensional scale model is a foolproof planning tool.

LIGHTING

There are many options to consider when planning your studio lighting. Natural light is ideal, but many basement and garage (and some apartment) studios do not have that access to the outside.

Overhead fluorescent lighting is a must in the woodshop. You are constantly reading rulers and scales on your machinery. When working with machinery, you need to see where your hands are. Installing 4' fluorescent lighting should be considered instead of the 8' variety. It is much safer and easier to change fluorescent bulbs when they are only 4' long. Fluorescent lighting fixtures should be placed every 10' to 12' to provide adequate lighting coverage.

Incandescent task lighting is a necessary addition to many dedicated task areas. The use of magnetically attached lighting on machinery such as the lathe, scroll, saw, drill press, band saw, and miter saw is ideal. Many lights have flexible necks and are easily adjusted to your needs.

Another important kind of lighting, especially when applying finish or sanding your work, is cross lighting. Wood carvers use cross lighting, which is lowering the angle of light so it shines across the work surface, to view their work. Cross lighting is a must when sanding or applying finish to your work. It is advisable to use a flood light reflector for this task. The multiple light sources can quickly reveal problem areas in your work.

Laying Out Your Shop

When planning the layout of your work area, make to-scale floor plans and same-scale equipment templates. Create a template for every piece of furniture, equipment, and fixture you plan to install, including storage for tools and materials. This way you can arrange and rearrange your layout without lugging the equipment back and forth in the shop. Use ¼" grid paper for the room size and cut out colored card stock to the same scale to represent your equipment.

Keep in mind your workflow when laying out the equipment in your shop. Lumber and plywood are difficult to handle in tight places.

Think about what you plan to do in your workshop, and what the most efficient arrangement would be. This level of planning ahead of time—accommodating logic and workflow—will save you a lot of time and streamline your work, making for a lot more fun in the woodshop.

MOBILITY

When your quarters are tight, making your machinery mobile gives you the most versatility. You can purchase aftermarket mobile bases for almost all machinery or you can make them by constructing wooden or metal platforms with heavy-duty casters attached. Make sure your casters have proper locking mechanisms.

ISOLATED MACHINE AREA

If you can isolate your machine area, that will help reduce the amount of noise and dust getting into your bench or assembly area. (If your basement shop has an open pilot light, be extra careful as fine dust or finishing fumes could be a serious problem.) Make sure the area is well ventilated by opening windows and using an exhaust fan.

Working in the basement can create noise that the rest of the family (or neighbors) may not enjoy. Adding insulation and a layer of drywall in the ceiling will help to muffle the noise. Checking and changing filters in the HVAC system will keep sawdust from clogging up the works.

ASSEMBLY AREA

When assembling your wood projects, it is handy to have a moveable workstation with carpet padding on the top surface. You will save hours of time trying to repair dings and scratches on your work that occurred while assembling your piece on an unpadded bench. It is also advisable to pad the top of your wooden horses with strips of carpet.

For example, if you are milling your own lumber there is a sequence to follow.

- The jointer and planer should be parallel to each other because you will flatten and square your boards first.
- There should be enough room on the side of the jointer for you to walk the boards through.
- As the boards go through the planer, you should have enough room to walk around to catch the board as it comes out of the planer.
- Leave enough room in back and in front of your machines to accommodate an 8' length of lumber or plywood. This should be planned for the table saw, jointer, and planer.
- The radial arm or miter saw should be placed in the same proximity to make cross cuts on the lumber.

AIR COMPRESSORS

Air compressors have an important role in the wood shop. They power brad and pin nailers as well as other accessories. Pneumatic tools are becoming more popular today, and air is a must if you plan to use spray paint or finishes. Thirty gallon or larger compressors can be installed as permanent fixtures in the shop. They are loud and can be muffled by enclosing them in a 1" foam-lined plywood box with vents for cooling. It would be ideal to pipe air throughout the shop. This can be done using black iron pipe or plastic tubing with connectors at various workstations. Your pneumatic tools can be quickly connected to these stations. Smaller compressors are portable and are ideal for the small shop.

RIGHT The portable compressor is a must when doing installations on location.

Storage

LUMBER STORAGE

You should create a dedicated area for storing your stash of lumber and sheet goods. Placing wood on your garage (or any concrete) floor is asking for trouble as wood will absorb moisture like a sponge. Horizontal storage shelves on your walls are ideal for keeping your lumber flat and accessible. Store your plywood vertically, resting on two-by-fours or a plastic tarp. Create a means for storing your lumber cut-offs. These little morsels can really clutter up the shop if not stored properly. A set of cubbies, a rolling storage bin, or even several drawers can help keep cut-offs orderly and easier to find.

> **TIP** **Cover That Buckle!**
>
> Keep your belt buckles and buttons covered up with an apron, as they can scratch or ruin beautiful finished pieces.

TOOL STORAGE

Too many hand tools can be a problem if you have no way to store them. I have been in shops where you could not see the workbench for the volume of hand tools strewn about. How you treat your tools will be reflected in your finished work, so always be mindful, organized, and deliberate.

Keep your bench uncluttered. All your tools should be organized and stowed in drawers, cabinets, shelves, and on hooks when they are not in use. For the hand tools you use the most, consider making a hanging tool cabinet. Every tool has its place and you know where to find it and where it should be returned.

 Clamp Storage

Many woodworking experts say you can never have enough clamps. It is important that you provide storage racks for your clamps by size and type. See the bottom half of the photo below for clamp organization ideas.

No matter how extensive your tool collection is, consider making a hanging tool cabinet to keep your workspace organized.

Visual Glossary of Shop Machinery

▼ A 16-32 **drum sander** will enable you to sand a table top 32" wide. The drum sander has a rotating drum that is wrapped with sandpaper. The moving platen carries the wood under the rotating drum. The platen can be adjusted up or down to accommodate the thickness of the piece being sanded. Different grits of sandpaper can be attached to the drum. It will sand 16" in one pass, then turn the piece and sand the other side. Notice the plywood and caster portable base.

▲ Shop-made **portable router table**. The on/off switch is located outside for safety. When in use it is hooked up to a wet/dry vacuum for dust control.

(continued on page 16)

Visual Glossary of Shop Machinery (continued)

▼ A 10" **miter saw** with extended sides allow the stable cutting of long boards. The top of the fence has a calibrated scale to enable quick, accurate, and repeatable cuts.

▲ The combination of the **jointer** and **surface planer** produce straight and flat lumber. The jointer is used to achieve a flat surface on one side of the board by eliminating any warping or bowing. Place the flattened side face down and send it through the planer. This will flatten the top of the board and make it parallel to the opposite side. Both of these machines can be easily connected to a dust collector using 4" hoses.

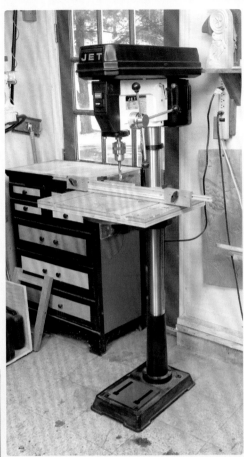

▼ This **band saw** is mounted on a portable base. By changing the saw blade to an ⅛" width, you can cut tight circles or other shapes. Using a wider blade, you can cut through a slab of wood 6" thick. The base contains storage for blades and accessories.

▲ A **floor standing drill press** can drill holes in wood and metal. The shop-made tabletop has tracks for a move-able fence and stop blocks. This fence system allows you to make repeatable drilling tasks. Changing the belt drives on the machine's internal pulley clusters allows for sixteen speeds. This particular drill press has a built-in internal light.

(continued on page 18)

Visual Glossary of Shop Machinery (continued)

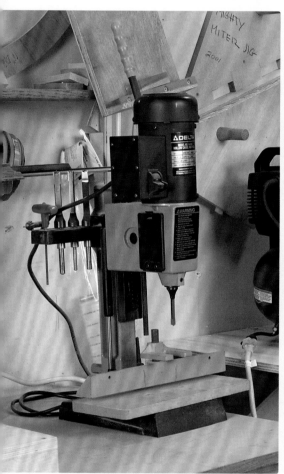

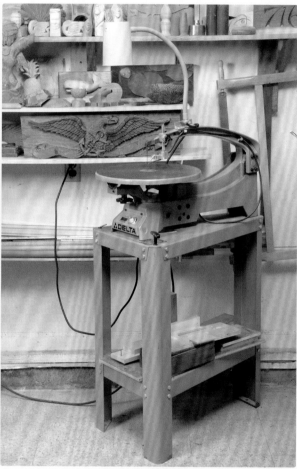

▲ **Bench-top mortising machine** chops mortises from ¼" to ½" square. This cut is made by a drill housed inside a sharp square chisel. The depth can be adjusted for shallow or deeper mortise slots. This machine is used when making mortise and tenon joinery. The rack on the left of the mortise holds the various sizes of chisels used in this machine.

▲ A **variable-speed scroll saw** is for very fine cutting on wood, plastic, and soft metals. With the proper blade, the saw is also capable of cutting wood up to 2" thick. The light attached is necessary for this type of close work.

Controlling Your Environment

NOISE CONTROL

Having your shop in your basement or attached garage means that machine noise can be a problem for your family or neighbors. Installing foam insulation can muffle a lot of the noise, alleviating the problem. Insulation can be placed in the ceiling of your basement, offering a reasonable sound barrier between your work space and the living space above. Rigid foam insulation can also be applied to walls and doors in garages and outbuildings. Before you install anything, check your fire codes. (Alternatively, another way to solve the noise problem is to only use hand tools!)

A dust collector can serve many different machines. The 10" table saw pictured here is permanently connected to the collector with a blast gate to regulate on or off use.

TIP **Remote Control Switch**

A remote control switch for activating your dust collector system is a great addition. This will save you time from running back and forth to the on/off switch.

DUST

Good dust control is essential in any woodshop. There are many makes and models of devices ranging from a small shop vacuum to large cyclone-style central air systems. The quantity and size of the machinery in your shop dictates your dust control needs.

For example, in my 1,200-square-foot shop I run an 8" jointer, a 15" planer, a 10" table saw, and a 16" drum sander, all using a 1½-hp dust collector. This size is adequate because I only collect from one machine at a time.

When working with palm sanding devices, try to hook them up to a shop vacuum. This will eliminate a lot of dust from clouding up your shop and getting into your lungs.

Ambient air cleaners, available in many sizes, are also a good addition to your shop. They hang from the ceiling and circulate the ambient air in the shop to collect fine airborne particles. They have a series of filters that can be changed when needed.

TIP | After the Dust Settles

Even with a good dust collection system, my shop still has dust settled all over the inside (along with many cobwebs). Several times a year, I open up the bay doors, put on my dust mask, and blast away at the dust with my leaf blower.

HEATING YOUR SPACE

If you live in a climate with cold or cool winters, heating your shop can be a challenge if it is not properly insulated. There are numerous ways to heat a shop, but your first efforts should be toward trying to insulate your work space as best you can. The investment in insulation will be returned with reduced heating costs over time.

Electric heat is very expensive. Overhead electric radiant heat is a better solution but it is still costly. Some woodworkers use portable kerosene heaters—this is not a recommended solution! A small propane furnace is adequate to heat up to a 1,000-square-foot area. If you have the budget and the space, a hot water radiant heat system in the floor is the ideal heating situation for a woodshop. This system could also be powered by a propane-fired furnace.

You can also use small forced-air furnaces with closed combustion chambers as well as propane or gas-fired radiant heaters.

If you have the space in your shop, a woodstove could be an excellent heating choice as long as it is properly installed. Each locale has strict codes for wood-fired stoves and the rules should be followed closely. Strategically placed fire extinguishers are good insurance against any mishaps.

COOLING YOUR SPACE

Hot, humid weather can be a problem in the wood shop, for both you and the lumber. An exhaust fan will help cool the air, but it does not eliminate humidity. A small wall-mounted air conditioner will help reduce humidity as well as cool a small shop. Change the filters of the air conditioner often as they will clog with sawdust.

A dehumidifier in the small shop will help to reduce moisture that could affect wood movement after a piece is assembled. As wood absorbs moisture it will expand. For example, if a solid wood door panel was set too tightly in a cabinet door, it will force the frame apart at the joint as the panel expands.

FLOORING

Standing for long hours on a cement floor can take a toll on your feet, legs, and back. Rubber or foam mats at each workstation can help ease fatigue. These mats also save the day (or the tool) when you accidentally drop a newly sharpened chisel.

If you have a cement floor, consider covering it with wood. First, cover the cement floor with plastic sheeting to act as a moisture barrier. Then, nail pressure-treated two-by-fours to the cement floor. Screw ¾" tongue-and-groove plywood to the two-by-fours. Another solution is to use interlocking plastic mats to cover cement areas.

Visual Glossary of Hand Tools

A well-equipped shop has a wide variety of hand tools. Depending on what you build, you may want to invest in many of these tools for yourself. Hand tools can also be rented from many home-improvement or hardware stores, or you can always borrow from fellow woodworkers in your network.

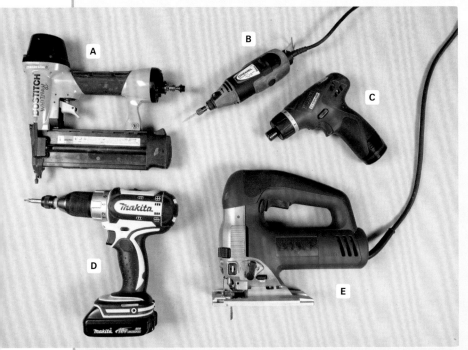

◀ **Battery, corded electric, and air powered hand tools**

A. Pneumatic brad nailer
B. Rotary tool
C. Battery-powered mini drill
D. Battery-powered heavy-duty drill/driver
E. Corded electric jigsaw

◀ **Different hammers for different jobs**

A. Wooden mallet used with carving chisels
B. Traditional claw hammer
C. Japanese hammer used to adjust plane blades
D. Non-marring dead blow hammer
E. Magnetic tack hammer used for upholstery
F. Beechwood mallet
G. Brass mallet for delicate tapping on carving chisels

(continued on page 22)

Visual Glossary of Hand Tools (continued)

▼ Hand planes

A. Back-pull Japanese plane
B. Bench plane
C. Handmade plane
D. Scrub plane for fast wood removal
E. Corner chisel plane
F. Block plane for delicate trimming
G. Shoulder plane
H. Edge trimming plane

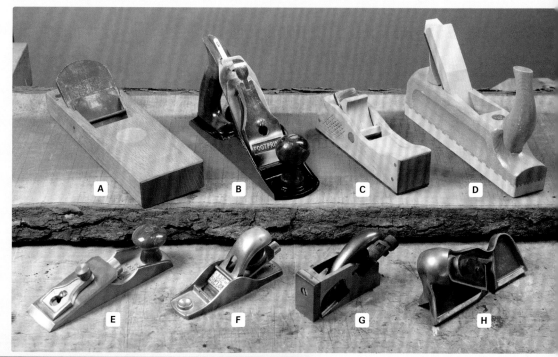

◀ Hand saws

A. Traditional backsaw for fine trim and dovetails
B. Delicate trim saw that uses changeable blades
C. Japanese ryoba combination rip and crosscut saw
D. Japanese dozuki backsaw or tenon saw
E. Japanese flush cut saw
F. Japanese dovetail saw that cuts a fine, thin kerf
G. Traditional crosscut saw

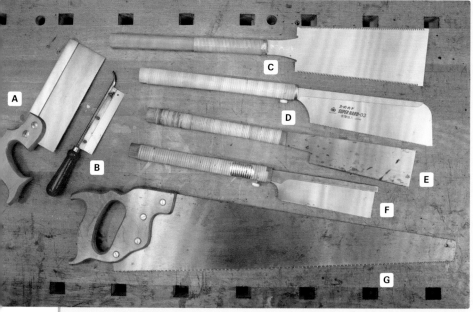

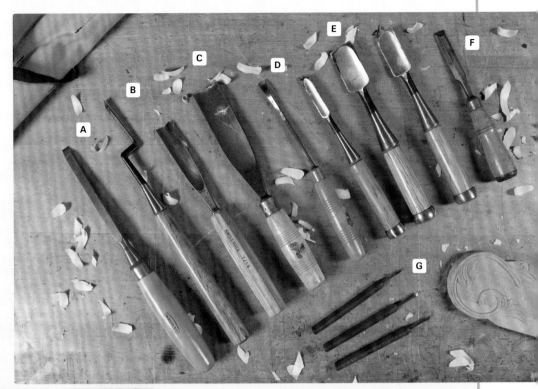

A dedicated sharpening station, below, keeps the mess away from the rest of the shop.

▲ **Chisels are made in many shapes and sizes to handle a variety of tasks.**

A. Mortise chisels are made to be tough, because they take a pounding.

B. Cranked-neck chisels reach hard to get places.

C. Carving chisels come in a variety of shapes and sizes.

D. Japanese skew chisel

E. Japanese bench chisels are laminated with hard and soft steel.

F. Flea market chisels can be brought back to life with some dedicated sharpening work.

G. Sets of miniature carving chisels are a necessity for fine detail.

If you have the room in your work area, setting up a dedicated sharpening station will save you a lot of time and keep you from messing up your workbench, as sharpening can become quite messy. Store your grinders, honing tools, and water or oil stones in this space.

(continued on page 24)

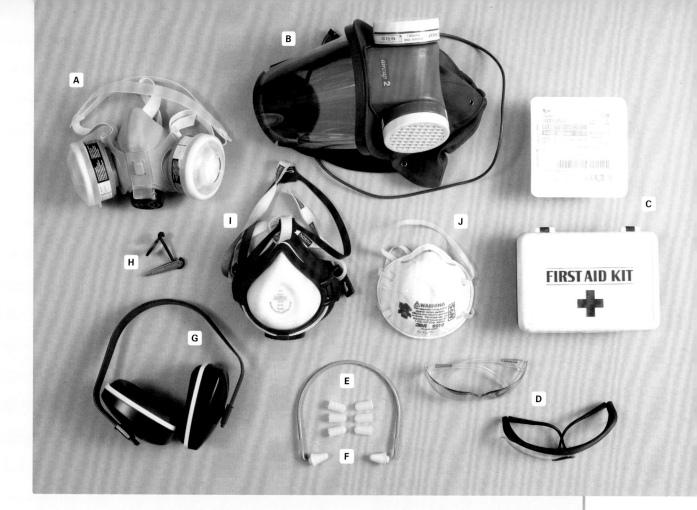

▲ **Using the proper safety protection offers you quality time while immersed in the joys of your woodshop.**

A. This face mask offers protection from vapors and fumes.

B. Battery-powered air filter and face shield attached to a hat, used for turning a lathe or sanding

C. Your first aid kit and large bandage packages are a must.

D. Safety glasses come in many shapes and sizes.

E. Disposable ear plugs are great for your friends watching you work.

F. Halo-style ear plugs

G. Ear muffs are comfortable hearing protection.

H. Tweezers with a magnifier are splinter fighters.

I. This dust mask offers changeable filters.

J. Disposable dust masks are readily available at your local hardware store.

Safety Considerations

Shop safety should be your biggest priority. Fingers and eyes don't grow back! A well-equipped first aid kit should be located in a convenient spot for quick access in case of emergency. Your cell phone should always be handy in case of a problem.

SAFETY EQUIPMENT

Safety glasses must be worn while you are using machinery of any kind. Face shields are an added safety measure when using lathes or grinders.

Lungs are also hard to replace! Proper dust masks should be used while using machinery that creates dust. The dust you don't see is the real danger. Fine micron particles are not easily filtered out by nose hairs. Even the best dust collection systems don't take away the fine dust that is so dangerous to our bodies.

Always protect your hearing by using ear plugs or ear muffs. All shop machinery is loud. Lack of proper hearing protection can cause you problems in the future.

Always keep a fire extinguisher on hand for managing solvent or electrical fires.

CAUTION: TABLE SAWS

Table saws, if not properly used, can be one of the most dangerous pieces of equipment in the wood shop.

- The use of push blocks and push sticks keep your fingers away from the spinning blade as you push the wood forward against the fence. Feather boards apply pressure to the wood and keep it tight against the fence. These aids are used to prevent kickback, which is one of the major causes of injury.
- Never wear gloves, as they are easily caught in the spinning blade. Button your cuffs or roll up your sleeves. Remove jewelry.
- Have an easily accessible cut-off switch that can be knee activated.
- Always lower the blade when your table saw is not in use.

There is a new type of table saw on the market called "SawStop." Its technology retracts the saw blade in a microsecond when it comes in contact with a finger or any other body part. Most of the newer table saws on the market have a riving knife attachment behind the blade that helps to prevent kickbacks. A riving knife or splitter prevents wood from moving into the blade as it is being ripped.

Be sure to also install the blade guard that comes with every table saw, whenever a cutting operation permits it. A blade guard protects you from accidental contact with the blade. You can also attach a dust collector hose to the blade guard.

NOTES OF GENERAL CAUTION

- Unplug the power source when changing blades on any piece of equipment.
- Keep your shop uncluttered. Pick up extension cords and stray lumber.
- Never leave your shop open when you are not there. Children are very inquisitive.

As your hobby or business grows, your list of questions on how to facilitate growth may grow too. With proper planning, you can turn available space into a comfortable, safe, and functional work area.

TIP | Before You Begin to Build

Not everyone starts out in woodworking with a fully equipped studio. When choosing a project to build, select one that you can build using the tools you have on hand. Choose wood that you don't have to mill if you don't have a jointer or planer available to you. Design or check your plans to determine what type of equipment is needed to start and complete the project.

The Wonders
of Wood

Have you ever bought a piece of furniture in a chain furniture store and found out later that it was not real wood? After close inspection, the wood grain vinyl that was covering up flake board carcase started to wrinkle and peel off. Maybe the legs started to wobble because the fasteners were tearing away from the particleboard. Mass-produced furniture may cost less, but the quality is questionable. These are the reasons we all want to build solid wood furniture. Solid wood furniture made centuries ago still lives today.

Wood Is Where You Find It

Wood used for making furniture or small objects can come from many sources. A trip to the home center, lumberyard, or even the firewood pile can yield treasures that will make your project outstanding. But what should you choose, and where will you find it?

As you drive by an industrial or commercial area, you may see wooden pallets placed on the curb. They may be made of knotty oak or low-quality pine. Some industrious woodworkers pick them up and produce creative pieces using this tough material. Years ago, shipping containers were made of lower grades of mahogany and teak wood. Once the nails were removed, this wood was a valuable resource for woodworkers. Today you have to go to the lumberyard to purchase these species.

The vast varieties of wood that abound throughout the world offer the woodworker treasures close to home, no matter where home is. There are more than 100 species of wood found in North America alone, for example. These species fall into two major categories: deciduous trees, which have leaves and are mostly hardwoods, and coniferous trees, also called evergreens, which have needles and are mostly softwoods.

Such a variety of wood offers the woodworker choices to fit every need. Soft woods such as the pine varieties are the most prevalent and versatile species. Pine is the major wood used in building construction. White pine has long been used for furniture, cabinets, trim work, and interior finishing.

Walnut, cherry, maple, and oak varieties are the most popular North American hardwoods used by cabinetmakers and furniture builders. These woods are also used in flooring and interior finishing. Tulip poplar is used as a secondary wood in making furniture, and its smooth grain is ideal for painting.

There are domestic woods that are impervious to weather, such as white oak, redwood, black locust, and a variety of cedars. These are used in boat building, outdoor furniture, siding, and fencing. Wood carvers look for woods such as basswood, butternut, clear white pine, black walnut, and cherry. Wood turners search for green or dried logs, burls, spalted birch, or maple for bowl work.

VISITING THE LUMBERYARD

You will not find most of these species in the local home center. You must search for certain species in sawmills, specialty lumberyards, woodworking periodicals, or on the Internet. The home center variety of lumber is commonly milled to ¾" thick. It comes in lengths from 4 feet to 12 feet and is often already surfaced and sanded smooth. The wood usually still has mill marks that have to be eliminated if you're using it for a high-end piece. The problem here is that by the time you get rid of the mill marks and sand the surface, you wind up with less than ¾" lumber. Check these boards for any warping or twisting, as this could yield a thinner plank by the time you mill it flat. These

stores usually carry about four species of lumber such as poplar, oak, aspen, and pine. The availability of species may vary by region.

If your needs are for additional species and thicker boards that you can mill yourself, these can be found at the larger lumberyards or sawmills.

Lumberyards carry many types (and grades) of lumber for construction, trim, and cabinet making. The species and sizes of wood are color coded for quick identification. Color coding differs from one lumberyard to the next to meet their own inventory needs.

Most lumber companies let you pick out the boards you need. Most of the boards are common widths and thicknesses. Boards are sold by the linear foot, while thicker rough-cut wood species are sold by the board foot (see page 29 for how to calculate the board foot).

What to Look for When Shopping for Wood

- Bring your lumber cut list to determine size and amount of lumber needed.
- Check for warps, twists, cracks, knots, or any other deformities that could compromise your needs.
- Check for matching grains and color when selecting wood of the same species.
- Make sure the wood that you purchase is kiln dried (KD).
- Choose board sizes that will give you the best economy.
- Make sure the wood is well protected from denting or scratching when transporting it back to your shop.

Stacks of lumber awaiting your inspection. They are color coded by species, grade, and thickness.

ROUGH-SAWN LUMBER

The species of wood needed for your project will determine what lumber source you use. Your local sawmill can provide most domestic hardwoods such as oak, cherry, poplar, walnut, or whatever is common to your region. If your need is for more exotic woods such as teak, bubinga, or mahogany, you will have to locate a specialty mill. These mills can be found on the Internet.

The advantage of purchasing rough-sawn lumber is you can mill to your own dimensions needed for your project. This is fine if you have a jointer and planer available. If not, your mill can dimension the wood for you.

When you purchase rough-milled lumber from your lumberyard or mill shop it is sold in thicknesses starting at 4/4 (1"). The thickness of lumber is measured in $\frac{1}{4}$" increments starting at four quarter, which is 1", up to 12/4, or 3". These measurements are accurate to the inch scale, unlike the well-known 2" × 4", which actually measures $1\frac{1}{2}$" × $3\frac{1}{2}$".

When purchasing rough-cut or "off the saw" lumber, you buy a thickness greater than the finished milled dimension. Random widths are calculated by the widest part of the plank. When milling your own wood, the extra thickness guarantees the final dimension. If the mill dimensions your wood, they will bill by the oversize dimension and probably charge for the milling time.

Rough-cut lumber at the mill is usually sold by the board foot. To determine the board feet of a plank, multiply the thickness × the width × the length, then divide by 144. A board foot is a measure of lumber volume. The mill uses the board foot measure because they have purchased the wood using the board foot equation. There is usually a lot of waste with rough-cut lumber that they have already purchased. This is passed onto the consumer. The linear dimension is used for already-milled lumber at the home stores and is charged by the length and width.

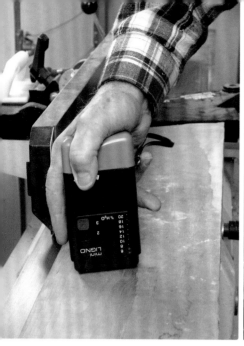

Check your lumber with a moisture meter to verify the moisture content. This can be done on end grain as well as on the board surface.

Flattening a severely warped board on the jointer will yield a board that may become too thin to use.

This warped 5/4 board will probably finish out to 1/2" or less after it is planed.

When purchasing wood from the sawmill, there are several things to consider.

First, make sure the lumber you are purchasing is kiln dried. You can easily check the moisture content of the wood you're selecting by using a moisture meter. If you are making furniture, be sure that the moisture content is between 6 and 10 percent.

Wood is like a sponge. It will absorb moisture as well as expel moisture according to the atmospheric conditions. Building solid wood furniture with wood that is not dried to 6 to 10 percent can lead to problems. Wood will continue to dry when in a heated room during the winter months. Wood will absorb moisture during the humid days of summer. This continual expansion and contraction is what loosens joints and splits tabletops.

Air-dried lumber is also acceptable, provided it was properly dried. Some woodworkers prefer air-dried stock because it retains better color and steam-bending properties.

Second, check for the flatness of the boards you select. Warped or wavy boards may not yield the thickness needed after a lot of jointing and planing.

Check the boards by eyeballing from one end to the other for any curvature. Use a combination square to check across the board for flatness. Having your lumber cut list is important at this time. If you are looking at an 8' board that has a slight curve, but it will be used to yield three 24" pieces, for example, a slight curve would be acceptable. Cutting the board into three equal pieces will minimize any curvature and allow you to mill to a proper thickness.

Third, check for color and grain match when selecting lumber. This is especially important if you are going to finish the piece in a natural finish. Color match is less important if you plan to stain or paint the piece. Color variations in lumber can translate into the finished piece. Be aware of knots and end checks or splits at the end of the boards.

And finally, allow for about 20 percent waste when ordering rough-cut lumber. There will always be end checks (splitting), sap wood (lighter wood next to the bark), grain matching, as well as the milling process itself to reduce the quantity of wood you've ordered. Keep in mind the need for some test cuts and maybe a mistake or two.

Plywood and Other Composite Panels

The home center selections of sheet goods or plywood are usually grades used for construction and building purposes. Some centers carry cabinet-grade plywood such as oak, birch, and maple as well as MDF. Care should be taken when selecting ¾" hardwood veneer plywood at home centers. These sheets tend to curve after they are pulled from the pile. Most of the better grades of plywood can be found in larger lumberyards. The wood cores have fewer voids or open spaces, they are more stable, and the outer layer of veneers are thicker. Most of the better grades of plywood are manufactured in Canada and the United States. You will pay a little more for them.

Some specialty lumber companies offer a variety of cabinet-grade plywood. These plywood have surfaces made from hardwood veneers such as cherry, walnut, quarter-sawn oak, bird's eye maple, and just about any other species you would need for your woodworking projects. Some of these specialty panels have a core of MDF with the wood veneer applied. The MDF panels assure a flat, smooth surface. Suppliers of these types of panels can best be found on the Internet or in woodworking magazines. These specialty plywood are very expensive, but they will yield superior effects for high-end projects.

Plywood and other sheet materials come in a variety of sizes, textures, shapes, and colors. Standard thicknesses range from ⅛" to 1" thick. These panels are stable and free from wood movement. They can be used in combination with solid woods to create furniture, cabinets, and architectural elements, such as large curved and oversized panels. Hardwood veneered plywood is the panel of choice for furniture makers.

Baltic birch plywood is the most stable of the plywood varieties. It is made with multiple veneer layers and is void free. The edges are more decorative and can be exposed, while other plywood edging should be banded to hide the irregularities. Baltic birch is very stable and is used to make jigs and fixtures.

Melamine-coated particleboard is coated with hard plastic. It provides a durable smooth surface. It is used in workshops for worktops and tables in front of table saws. Particleboard is not ideal for screw holding as it tears and crumbles easily.

Prefinished cabinet-grade plywood is used in making kitchen and laboratory cabinets. It is prefinished on one side, usually with a lacquer. This surface is placed on the inside of the cabinet and eliminates any need for further finishing.

MDF has a flat smooth surface. This makes it ideal for a painting surface or applying veneer. A 4' × 8' × ¾" sheet of this material is very heavy and is hard to maneuver by one person. When exposed to moisture it swells irreversibly.

A cutting list (see page 48) is essential for planning your cuts. Instead of maneuvering heavy, large panels in a crowded workshop, you can ask associates at the lumberyard to cut 4' × 8' sheets of plywood to your desired dimensions. It also can make for easier transport home if you don't have a truck.

TIP Rough-Milled Lumber Grain

To get an idea of what the grain looks like on rough-milled lumber, pour some water or mineral spirits on a small area and rub out with a rag. This will give you a good visual of the potential look of the grain.

▲ **There are many types of plywood and manmade panels for many different applications. Pictured here:**

A. ½" hardwood veneer-core plywood with oak face

B. Prefinished hardwood veneer-core plywood with birch face

C. ¾" hardwood core plywood with oak face

D. Baltic birch plywood

E. Solid-core MDF with walnut face

F. MDF

G. Particleboard

H. Particleboard with melamine face

 I. Masonite or hard board

▲ When cutting plywood on your table saw or miter saw, a fine-tooth, sharp blade must be used to help eliminate the tear out on the underside of your plywood. A zero-tolerance insert plate on the table saw should eliminate this type of destruction. Place a thin piece of hard board, such as Masonite, under the plywood when cutting on the miter saw. This will eliminate the tear out.

LEFT The panel saw, such as this one at Kuiken Brothers Lumber Yard in Wantage, New Jersey, makes quick work of cutting heavy sheets of plywood to size. The saw can be adjusted to cut horizontally or vertically.

RIGHT The cut panels are smaller and easier to handle.

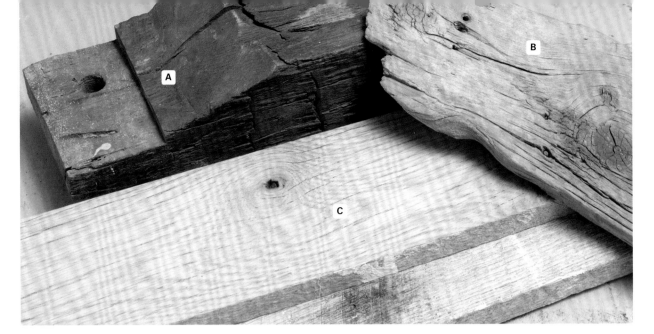

Old chestnut hand-hewn barn beams (A), weathered barn siding (B), and red oak planks (C) are great sources of old-growth wood. Look out for nails!

Recycled Wood

Furniture made from recycled or reclaimed wood is gaining favor and is the "green" (or ecologically friendly) way to conserve our steadily depleting wood supply. There is too much wood that finds its way to the landfill instead of being recycled and used to create beautiful woodwork. A lot of extremely valuable wood, such as chestnut, walnut, and mahogany, comes from old building renovations and demolitions. To buy these species of new wood today would cost a fortune. (Blight has wiped out the chestnut trees in North America, for example, so recycled chestnut is a particular prize.)

Wood recycling companies thrive on reclaiming flooring, beams, doors, windows, and trim work. Other businesses specialize in reclaiming lumber from old barns and even factories. Some old factory floorboards are 2" thick! Most of the wood reclaimed is old-growth lumber, and it is the most stable wood available today. Weathered barn siding makes beautiful tabletops, even though they may show years of weathering and a few nail holes.

When selecting old wood from a depleted barn or building, always check for dry rot, termite infestation, and hidden metal objects. Scanning boards with a metal detector can save your saw blades from cutting through screws or nails. Putting small pieces of wood in the microwave for just 30 seconds is a quick way to stop bug infestation!

TIP | Growth Rings

In dense forests, trees grow very slowly. The growth rings of these trees are very close together, which makes the wood very stable. This recycled lumber is expensive, but it can yield beautiful results.

Another type of recycled lumber is old-growth logs that have been submerged under water for 100 years or more. Typically, this lumber was "lost" in transporting logged trees. There are salvage companies that specialize in bringing these sunken treasures to the surface. The enormous benefit of this lumber is that on the bottom of a body of water, they lay entombed, unable to decay because of lack of oxygen. Another similar source of "tree treasures" is peat bogs, where ancient logs have slept for thousands of years. Port Orford cedar and cypress, to name a couple, are often obtained in this fashion.

Veneers and Exotic Wood

Most exotic woods come from Africa, South America, and Asia. Many of them are on the endangered species list. They are expensive and hard to come by. Most of these beautiful logs are milled and sliced to make veneers. This is the only way to ration some of the disappearing rain forest varieties, such as rosewood, purple heart, lacewood, wenge, bubinga, and padauk.

Examples of highly figured wood are bird's eye maple, curly maple, madrone, redwood burls, quarter-sawn white oak, and sycamore. Crotch wood veneers can be book-matched (see page 70) or opened up facing each other to yield startling results. They yield feather and flame grains that are used in door panels.

To achieve the look of solid wood, apply veneer to plywood, MDF panels, or secondary wood such as poplar and pine. Veneers can be applied to the panels with glue using a veneer press or vacuum-forming system. When applying veneers to any surface, you

▲ **The wide varieties of veneers that are available will enable you to create some breathtaking, exciting work. Above:**

A. quilted cherry
B. curly maple
C. bird's eye maple
D. rosewood

◄ **Examples of imported exotic woods:**

A. rosewood
B. purple heart
C. Madagascar ebony
D. teak
E. mahogany

An Exotic Desk

At the time of this writing, I was commissioned to build an 80" × 40" desk using a 2½" thick slab of African bubinga. The client saw a sample of the wood on Hearne Hardwoods' website and decided that was the plank around which he wanted me to design the desk. The grain on the piece was too beautiful to pass up. The original plank was 170" long by 55" wide. The plank looked beautiful online, but with this kind of investment, I made the 200-mile trip to the lumberyard to examine it firsthand. The yard was quite accommodating and assigned a worker with a forklift to help me explore the stickered log of bubinga. We sifted through several planks before I found the correct one for the project.

The lumber company cut the desktop to the approximate size and rough-sanded it at their facility. The planks were shipped by truck to my studio. It took five strong men to unload the 400-pound desktop and the other half of the plank. The cost of this rare wood was in the thousands of dollars.

Slabs of bubinga rest on the studio floor. Note the amazing grain.

must apply a backer veneer to the opposite side of the board to equalize the drying process. If this were not done, the board would bow. Veneers can be applied to curved or irregular surfaces.

Exotic hardwoods from around the world are still available at specialty lumber companies. Unfortunately, the prices can also be exotic. These lumber companies have owners or staff who travel the world searching for this wooden gold. Some of the trees are shipped back as whole logs, while others are sawn and shipped in a stickered boulé. A boulé is a log sliced into boards, with the boards placed back in the order in which they were cut. This way boards can be matched to each other for consistent color and grain. When the logs reach the mill, they are sawn into planks, stickered, kiln dried, and stored in large sheds. (Most of the planks are photographed and displayed on the company website, because they are such prized offerings.)

A good way to begin using exotic or highly figured wood is to build a small box, which highlights its beautiful details and maximizes small quantities. (See page 68 in chapter 4.)

Buying exotic and highly figured wood has become a lot easier as dealers have started websites. Some dealers have minimum price schedules, while others will ship small orders. Online auction sites offer a large selection of wood sold by independents and small dealers. Care should be taken that what you see is what you really get!

ABOVE, LEFT A giant oak tree felled by a severe wind storm. (Photo by David Hill.)

ABOVE, RIGHT In this case, a friend asked me if I would like to have this gigantic red oak that had fallen on his house. His tree service removed the tree from his house and cut the trunk into 8' lengths for me. These sizes made it easier to transport them back to my woodshop. (Photo by David Hill.)

RIGHT Dick Plog, my sawyer, slices a log with a portable band saw mill. (Photo by Andy Schmidt.)

Wood Lot and Backyard Lumber

Being able to mill your own wood is a great way to save money on lumber purchases. There are many ways to acquire logs to cut. You can establish a connection to a tree service, become friendly with the road department, find (or inherit) a wood lot to cut from, or have a neighbor's tree fall on your house!

I do not mean to make light of such disasters, but a lot of wood becomes available when storms wreak havoc on communities and large limbs or trees are felled by the weather.

HOW TO HARVEST LOGS

- When you acquire logs to harvest, place them on 4" × 4" boards to keep them off the ground and away from moisture until you are ready to cut them.
- Paint the ends of the logs with leftover paint or other suitable green wood–stabilizer to seal the end grain. This will slow checking or splitting on the ends.
- There are several ways to turn your logs into lumber. You can take them to a lumber mill and have them sawn. You can have a sawyer come to your location with a portable band saw mill. Or there are attachments to allow you to use a chainsaw to slice up the logs. Any of these methods will allow you to cut your lumber to any thickness desired.

AIR-DRYING CUT LOGS

Now that the lumber is cut, it has to be dried. A rule of thumb for calculating the air-drying time for lumber is one year per inch of thickness. This will still not get the lumber to the 6 percent moisture level needed for making furniture. Ideally, the drying process for cut lumber could be finished in a kiln for about thirty days. The stickered boards could be moved indoors to a warmer atmosphere for a few months. This should hasten the drying process. Do not apply heat directly to lumber, because the heat will warp and split your treasure.

Stickers are made from almost any wood that is dry. Ripped into ¾" square strips, they are cut to length to match the width of the boards they are separating. They should be placed evenly across the lumber every 18" to 24". As you sticker each layer, the stickers should align with the previously placed stickers. Stickering allows air to evenly circulate between the lumber. Placing stickers too far apart will allow the boards to sag and become wavy.

Stacking green, wet lumber without stickering will cause the lumber to mildew or rot because there is no way to dispel the moisture.

WOOD PILE TREASURES

Partially rotting burls or crotch pieces can yield striking grain when resawn and book-matched (see page 70). Maple and birch logs will start to spalt as a fungus begins to take over the log. The spalting process leaves spidery black lines that randomly creep their way through the wood. A log that is starting to show these black lines should be cut into boards, and the drying process should be started. If this is not done, the log will continue to decompose.

Wood turners especially find that the woodpile contains a treasure trove of green or decaying logs that can be shaped into vessels and bowls.

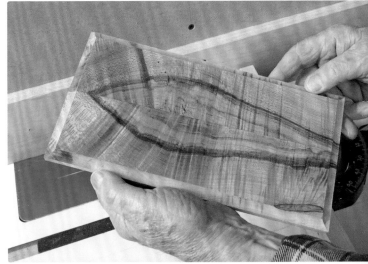

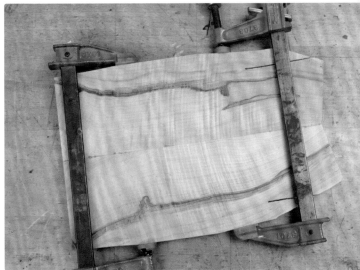

LEFT The beauty of spalted maple made this box an award-winner.

ABOVE, TOP Another example of a piece of maple that was resawn, book-matched, and glued together to make a box top.

ABOVE, BOTTOM A cut-off end of a maple plank was resawn and some striking rays as well as some fungus growth was exposed. The pieces were jointed and glued and clamped. This piece will be planed and later become the top for a box.

How to Prepare 8' Boards for Air Drying

1. Spread a tarpaulin on the ground to retard moisture absorption.

2. Build a level base with two ten-foot 6" × 6" treated wood planks placed 6' apart. Concrete blocks or bricks can be used to level these planks.

3. Lay five 4" × 4" × 7' timbers equally spaced across the base planks. Now you should have a level, solid base to sticker your boards onto. Eight-foot corrugated plastic or metal roofing panels can be attached on top of the stickered wood if there is not a covered area to store the pile. There are many articles and websites covering the topic of air-drying lumber. Some woodworkers prefer air-dried lumber; others prefer kiln-dried wood.

TIP | **Air-Drying Success**

Novice woodworkers should do additional research on air-drying lumber before diving in and drying a log's worth of lumber if they want to end up with suitable furniture lumber.

ABOVE, TOP The stickered lumber is under cover and waiting to dry. (Note the level, stable base.)

ABOVE, BOTTOM Air-dried planks are moved into the top of the barn to finish the drying process. A large exhaust fan is used to circulate the air and reduce the heat buildup under the roof.

MILLING THE WOOD

When your lumber has dried and you have designed your project, it is time to mill the wood. If you have boards with randomly shaped edges on each side, there are several ways to establish a straight edge.

1. For long boards, snap a chalk line on one side of the plank. Follow this line with a circular saw to trim a straight edge. Run this edge on the jointer or hand-plane it flat.

2. Use a straight edge to draw a straight line on the edge and follow it on a band saw. Again, joint the edge.

3. To trim planks that are 5' or less, screw a straight 3" or wider strip of plywood to one side of the plank. Run the edge of the plywood against the fence on the table saw. This will cut a clean straight edge to the other side of the board.

Now that a straight edge has been established, boards can be cut and milled to the dimensions on your cutting list.

Cut a straight edge on the plank using the table saw.

Project
Design

Whether you're building a birdhouse or remodeling a room in your home, any project needs planning and design to achieve great results. Some woodworkers purchase plans to build a piece of furniture, while others design and draw their own plans. Your ideas can start with rough sketches that can then be refined to final detailed plans. Early, thorough planning will help you decide the form, style, and type of wood you will need for your project.

There are thousands of plans available for projects ranging from boxes to beds. Every month, woodworking magazines feature free plans, and woodworking websites sell plans as well as videos that show the step-by-step methods for building a project. Beginning with existing plans can help you learn how to design and make your own plans in the future.

Start with your sketchbook
to capture your ideas.

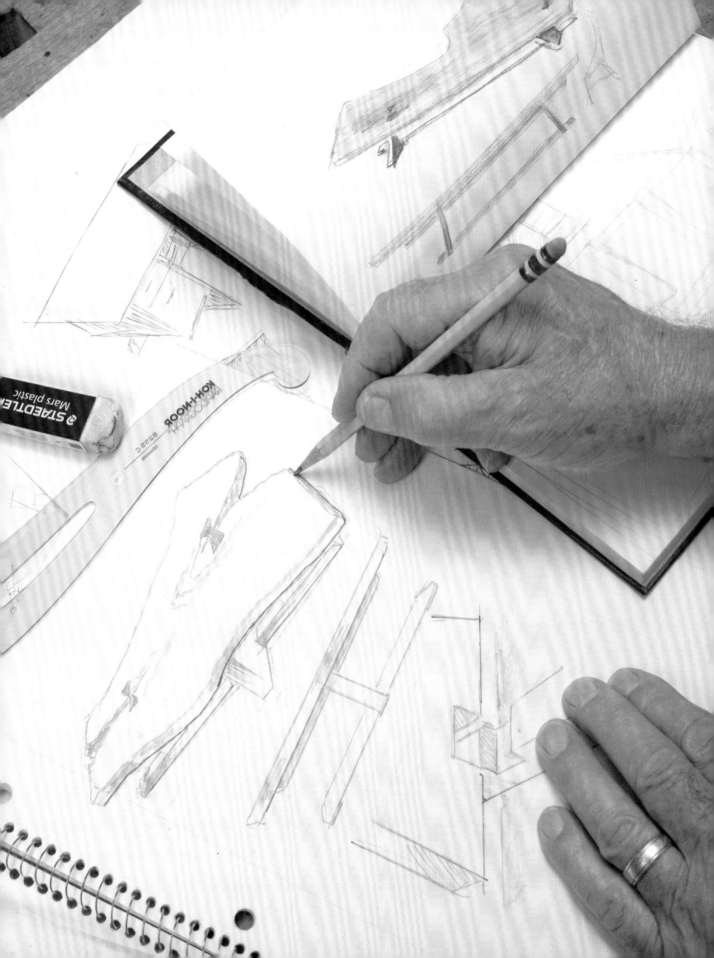

When planning or designing your own project, there are many styles and environmental considerations as well:

- **Aesthetic:** Does the style and finish of your project need to match other pieces in the room?
- **Dimensions:** Is there an area of your home or a room in which your project must fit, or be moved in and out of?
- **Sunlight:** Will your piece be subjected to direct sunlight? This will have a bearing on what type of finish you use.

- **Accommodation by interior features:** If your project will fit against a wall, you must be aware of the size and thickness of baseboards, and whether the floor and wall are square and level. Heating, air-conditioning ducts, and electrical outlets must be planned around, too.
- **Cost of materials:** Can your budget handle the cost of building with solid wood, choosing hardware, and purchasing any equipment needed to complete the project? Maybe you should consider building with pine or oak rather than more expensive walnut or cherry. Using plywood in combination with some solid wood could reduce your costs considerably.

Pyramid jewelry box made of slacked plywood and cherry.

Getting Started with Design

Start your planning process with the givens, such as the space your piece is to occupy. Furniture design or architectural standards books are good reference tools for learning the standard measurements for all types of furniture. With these references you can learn that desks, for example, are usually 29" to 30" high.

CASE STUDY: BOOKSHELVES

A lot of beginners start out making bookshelves. Building bookshelves seems simple enough, but careful planning is important. There are three basic types of materials for this project: solid wood, plywood, or medium-density fiberboard (MDF) composite wood.

If you plan to paint the shelves, MDF is a good choice because of its smooth, even surface. However, shelves made from MDF can sag, especially if they are longer than 28". You may want to consider solid wood or plywood for the shelves.

Building with ¾" plywood can give you a more stable set of shelves. You will have to plan on edge banding (see page 73) the exposed edges of the plywood. This can either be done with solid wood facing or iron-on veneer. Solid wood construction is the ideal for stability and overall appearance.

Once you have decided on what material will be used for the shelves, you must decide how they will be joined. How will the shelves be supported? Will they be adjustable shelves or fixed shelves? How will the top and bottom be joined to the vertical sides? What type of finish will be used? Will molding be used for the top and base? All of these questions have to be addressed before making your first cut.

CASE STUDY: CABINETS

There are also many questions to be answered when designing cabinets for the kitchen or den. Traditional cabinets are usually designed with face frames, which are made of solid wood and are a decorative way to conceal the plywood or MDF edges of the cabinet box. The hinges of the cabinet doors are secured to the face frame. The doors can be flush to the face frame or overlap.

Plywood Thickness

Plywood thickness can be misleading. For example, ¾" plywood is not really ¾" thick; ½" or ¼" plywood don't match their measurements either. Care should be taken when laying out a piece with multiple layers or sections of plywood. Four pieces of ¾" plywood does not add up to 3", because each board's thickness is really $^{23}/_{32}$". This could lead to a discrepancy of as much as ⅛". Half-inch plywood is actually $^{32}/_{64}$" thick, and ¼" is really $^{15}/_{64}$". When you glue ¾" solid-wood edge banding to ¾" plywood, the solid wood will be $^{1}/_{32}$" thicker than the plywood. This difference can be carefully sanded or planed off so the veneer on the plywood is not compromised.

Plywood Thickness (as labeled)	Actual Plywood Measurement
¼"	$^{15}/_{64}$"
½"	$^{32}/_{64}$"
¾"	$^{23}/_{64}$"

Planning your face frames leads to choosing the type of hinges to be used. Traditional brass hinges require mortises, or recesses, to house the hinge flap cut into the frame and the door. The Euro-style hinge (page 60) is hidden and offers great versatility both in adjustment and the type of closure. There are many other styles of hinges such as knife hinges, concealed barrel hinges, and so on. Information about available hardware can be found in woodworking catalogs and online. Learning about the options for each project is an important part of design and planning.

This type of planning for each project can save time and money as well as allow you to achieve a piece to be proud of.

USING YOUR SKETCHBOOK

Keeping a sketchbook or series of sketches is an essential part of designing. As ideas come to mind, always record them, even if it's on a napkin. (And you don't need more than rudimentary drawing skills to take notes of your ideas.) Drawing and sketching your ideas will help to increase your conceptual skills. Refinements to your ideas can be made on an ongoing basis in the sketchbook. Keep all your sketches (even the napkins); they will become a record of your progress. The sketches can then be honed and turned into working drawings.

TIP **Sketching Tips**

- Spiral-bound notebooks are ideal for sketching as they can be folded in half without breaking the binding.
- Always label your sketches and ideas with a title and a date.
- Your drawings can be made with pencils, pens, markers, or a combination. You don't have to be a Michelangelo, or even a trained artist, to sketch good ideas. Tools such as plastic circle guides, French curves, a compass, and, of course, a ruler can help you display your ideas.

REFERENCE SOURCES

Maintaining a library of reference books and magazines is invaluable for getting ideas and keeping up with trends in the woodworking arena. Woodworking enthusiast websites offer hundreds of fresh new ideas in design concepts, tips, and new joinery techniques every month. You can order how-to DVDs and plans from these sites that will help build your skills.

Trips to museums, galleries, and craft shows are another great way to get your creative juices flowing. Craft centers offer woodworking classes that are usually taught by expert woodworkers. Some classes may only be a day or two (usually on the weekend), while others can be two-week intensives. The size of the project determines the length of the class. Working in this type of atmosphere sends you back to the shop energized and determined to start on the next piece. There are many woodworking clubs and guilds that have woodshops available on a membership or fee basis. By enrolling in classes or clubs, you reap the benefits of having a group of like-minded craftspeople with whom you can discuss your ideas.

LEFT The author drew same-size plans using a ¼" piece of MDF for his drawing board.

ABOVE Maintain a good reference library, such as these shelves of well-organized books and magazines.

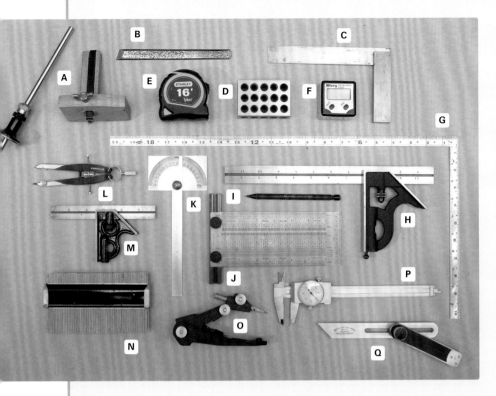

A good set of marking and drafting tools are essential for accuracy.

- **A.** Marking gauges
- **B.** Marking knife
- **C.** Engineer's square
- **D.** 1" × 2" × 3" set up block
- **E.** Tape measure
- **F.** Digital angle gauge
- **G.** Japanese square
- **H.** 12" combination square
- **I.** Mechanical pencil
- **J.** Incra T rule
- **K.** Engineer's protractor
- **L.** Compass
- **M.** 6" combination square
- **N.** Profile gauge
- **O.** Edge scribe
- **P.** Fractional dial caliper
- **Q.** Sliding bevel gauge

Drawing Your Plans

After making rough sketches, start your drawing using ¼" grid paper. Assign a measurement to each square so your drawings are scaled accurately. A quarter inch equals 1' is an easy way to scale your drawing. Drawing on grid paper is easy because you don't need a lot of drafting tools.

You should draw at least three views of your project. The front, side, and top views will give you a good preview of what your finished project will look like.

This is a good opportunity to draw individual parts of your project, such as legs, aprons, doors, frames, tops, sides, and so on, on the grid paper. Each part should be assigned a description, a number, and dimensions. These indications can now be applied to a lumber cutting list.

Making same-size drawings of the joinery is necessary to eliminate mistakes in the future.

DRAFTING TOOLS

A set of drafting, measuring, and marking tools is essential for drawing your same-size plans. These plans can be drawn on a large sheet of paper taped to your workbench or to a piece of plywood. Large rolls of craft paper can be purchased at office supply stores and are ideal for drawing. You can also draw your plan directly on a sheet of ¼" plywood or MDF. After your project is finished, the pencil marks can be erased so you can reuse the panels when drawing your next project.

- A **marking gauge** is used to transcribe dimensions onto wood. They can mark where to cut mortises, tenons, or dovetails.

- A **marking knife** is also used to transfer dimensions onto wood. One side of the marking knife is flat, which makes it easy to hold against a shape as you scribe.

- The **fractional caliper** is used for measuring the thickness of boards as well as the inside and depth dimensions.
- **Combination squares** and **framer squares** ensure accurate drawing and are used for checking for squareness.
- The **compass** is used to draw circles and arcs, while an **engineer's protractor** can accurately find an angle or create one to be transcribed to a drawing. Both are quite useful for same-size drawings.
- The **sliding bevel gauge** is used to transfer angles to drawings or materials.

If you have good drafting skills, you may want to draw an exploded view of your project to help visualize how the piece is assembled. An exploded view shows all of the pieces in a project separated in order of their proper position before they are assembled. Exploded views are usually drawn in isometric (three-dimensional without perspective) or perspective. They are frequently used to give you a good visual of how to put the project together. The exploded view does not have to be drawn same size. Exploded views can also help a client or coworker visualize the project you are making.

The sketching and drafting process is a good way to conceive of and prepare for the construction of your woodworking pieces. Difficult joinery techniques can be drawn and redrawn until any problems are solved. Taking the time to sketch and resolve your construction problems on paper saves messing up valuable wood later.

After you have finished building your project, it is good practice to keep the plans for reference. You may want to build a similar piece in the future.

USING THE COMPUTER FOR DRAWING PLANS

There are many software programs available for drawing and drafting for the home woodworker that you can use to design a piece of furniture or a whole room plan. The learning curve on these programs may take time but the results are impressive. (Besides, more and more design work is being done on computers and will continue to be in the future.) Many commercial woodshops are using CNC (computer numerically controlled) programs and routers to produce furniture parts and carvings.

If you are looking to explore your options first, there are free 3D programs on the internet (such as Google SketchUp) that enable you to draw and design both in plan and perspective views. These allow you to experiment with computer drafting without making a significant purchase.

As 3D computer-aided drawing (CAD) programs such as SketchUp become more popular and accessible to woodworkers, there are also tutorial resources available to help you learn how to use them. Several woodworking magazines offer these tutorials either as online or DVD purchases. Furthermore, plans are being shared over the Internet. This offers another avenue for projects, project ideas, and a good opportunity to learn from fellow woodworkers.

Today, most of the technical and trade schools teach drafting on the computer exclusively while traditional drawing is becoming a lost art. All the more reason not to give up your sketching!

TIP | **Cutting Diagrams in CAD**

Another advantage to using a CAD program is that you can draw cutting diagrams quickly, easily, and accurately to lay out parts or to take to the lumberyard when shopping for lumber or sheet goods.

OPPOSITE This model, made from rough sketches, was constructed with plywood and hot-melt glue at ⅛ scale.

Building Scale Models and Prototypes

Building scale models of your ideas or designs can help you visualize the piece from many angles. These models can be life size or scaled-down versions. They can be made from poster board, foam core, plywood, or corrugated cardboard. Tape or hot-melt glue can be used to connect these materials. What looks good on paper doesn't tell the whole story. Making models can correct mistakes not seen in your drawings.

Even crude prototypes can help you see how much physical space a piece may take or how it synthesizes with other furniture or aspects of a room. It is much cheaper to prototype a new design than commit wood and other resources to building it only to discover mistakes or limitations that could have been prevented. While the commitment of time and energy to prototyping might delay the gratification of actually building the project, it's usually worth the effort to solidify your designs first for maximum payoff.

Scaled-down clay models can be created and used as reference by woodcarvers in making their sculptures. These models give you a view from all sides instead of looking at a one-dimensional drawing on paper.

Creating a Cutting List

Another essential component of the planning and design process is creating a cutting list. The cutting list allows you to accurately estimate material quantities so you can purchase the correct quantity and dimensions of lumber and sheet goods. This ensures you will make your cuts with a minimum of waste for maximum efficiency. (A cutting list is often called a material list.)

Every cutting list should include the piece/component name and at least two sets of dimensions for each piece: rough dimensions and final dimensions. The cutting list template included in Appendix II (see page 168) is an excellent way to organize yourself during the planning and design process.

MILLING YOUR OWN LUMBER

If you have the necessary equipment, such as a jointer and planer, to mill your own lumber, it is a good idea to mill your lumber oversize and let it acclimate in your shop for a few days. Stresses, such as cutting, cause changes within the wood. It will also acclimate to the humidity or lack thereof in your shop. The acclimation process should take up to a week, according to the thickness of the lumber. It is also a good idea to put pieces of wood between each layer (a process called stickering) to allow air to circulate.

Once it has settled, you can mill the wood to the final dimensions on your cutting or materials list. It is essential that you number each piece to correlate to the cutting list. This numbering can be done using chalk, tape, or pencil.

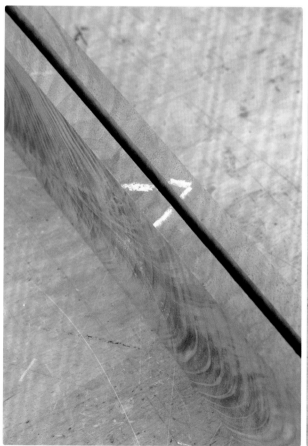

ABOVE (both) Witness marks help you control wood parts orientation.

Witness marks, which show orientation of matching pieces, can be applied to your wood using chalk, china markers, or pencils. Felt tip markers should not be used because the ink is difficult to remove.

One reliable way to plan your cuts is to use ¼" grid paper to sketch a cutting plan to scale. Plan all cuts on sheets of plywood to save a lot of wasted wood. Most plywood comes in 4' × 8' sizes. Draw out your measurements before cutting to ensure you can get the best yield from the plywood sheet. You can then transfer the accurate cutting dimensions to the plywood with pencil or chalk.

 TIP | **Waste Not, Want Not**

When ordering unmilled wood from the lumberyard, figure in 20 to 25 percent waste; so order 20 to 25 percent more wood than your plans call for. This should allow for knots, bad edges, and checks at the ends of the boards. Also, examine your lumber carefully before you bring it home. Look for grain match and consistent color before you commit to the wood.

ABOVE This arts and crafts-style lamp was an intricate design challenge. The segmented shade frame was made from walnut and rosewood with lacewood veneer applied. The octagon shape on the top and bottom of the shade needed precise angles to be cut. The vertical strips needed a compound angle cut to meet the top and bottom rims of the shade. All of this was carefully laid out on paper first. Test cuts were made. Support jigs had to be made to support the frame while being glued up.

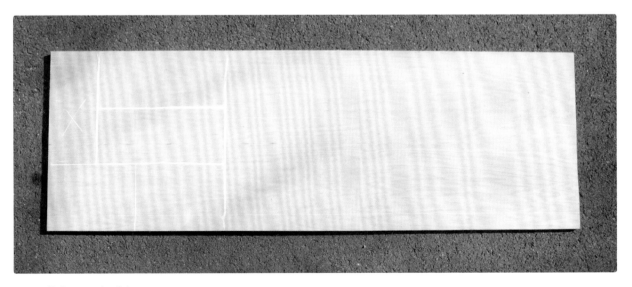

ABOVE Mark your rough-cut sizes on plywood panels with chalk.

CHAPTER

4

Wood
Joinery

When you were young, you may have had the pleasure of working with Dad or Grandpa in his work space. Maybe that was where you learned that joining wood using just hammer and nails isn't the best way to keep your projects together. Now that you have your own workshop, you have the challenge of choosing the joinery that will best hold your piece together, and that will suit your project the best. Some joints, such as dowel joints, conceal how the joint is fastened, and some don't. And some joinery styles, such as the popular dovetail or box joint, can even be exposed and decorative.

The projects in this chapter were selected because they show a variety of joinery techniques that can be adapted to many types of projects: intricate, simple, and everything in between.

Some of the projects in this book are slanted towards the beginner, while others are best suited for an intermediate level of experience. In the previous chapters you will have learned how to work with wood, how to select wood, and how to design. In this chapter you will learn how to join the wood together.

COMMON TECHNIQUES:
Joinery

The most common joinery technique is the butt joint, in which two pieces of wood are nailed together at a 90-degree angle. There are a few ways to reinforce the butt joint and make it secure.

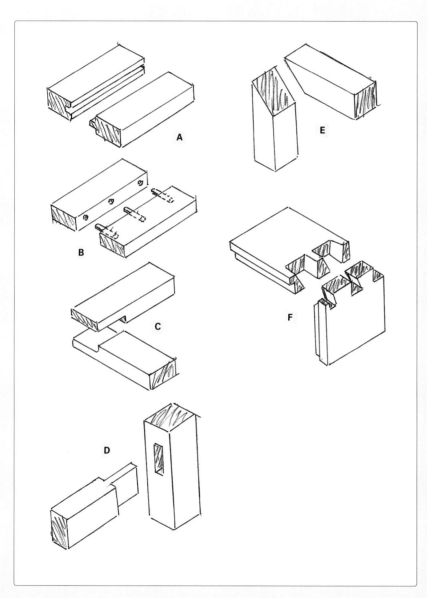

◄ **Common ways to join wood:**

A. tongue and groove joint
B. dowel joint
C. half lap joint
D. mortise and tennon joint
E. miter joint
F. dovetail joint

The author's sketches of different joinery configurations.

1

2

NAILS

It can be nailed together. This doesn't give much strength, because the nail passes through one board and into the end grain of the mating board. Additional strength could be added by using glue, but in time the joint will twist or move.

SCREWS

A power brad nailer can be used to secure the butt joint in place before screwing. This simply acts as a holding maneuver before screwing the joint together. You will increase the danger of the wood splitting if the screw holes are not predrilled.

Once the panels are cut to size, apply glue to the top and bottom edges and butt to the side panels. Clamp them together so they are square and flush. You can use right angle corners with clamps or a framing square.

Predrill the holes for the screws with a tapered drill bit that has a countersink head attached. This will allow for the screw heads to be driven in flush to the plywood sides. This will make a strong butt joint. This type of joinery is used when making kitchen cabinets.

1. Predrill the holes before screwing together a butt joint.

2. Secure the joint at right angles using a right angle corner with clamps. Proceed to drive the screws home.

(continued on page 54)

Joinery (continued)

The best way to secure and strengthen a butt joint is an interior device. These interior devices include dowels, biscuits, splines, and pocket hole screws. The dowel, spline, and biscuit joints gain their strength by creating additional glue surfaces that lock the butt joint together. End grain on the edge of a board does not make a strong glue joint.

DOWELS

1. To make an accurate dowel joint, you must first align the mating boards and register the joint with scribe lines across each piece using a square and pencil. These lines are used to align the doweling jig to each board.

2. The self-centering doweling jig clamps over the edge of the wood and aligns with the register marks. The jig has a series of standard diameter holes to guide the drill. In this case it's ⁵⁄₁₆", the same as the diameter of the dowels.

3. Insert the dowels with glue and clamp them together to make a tight, accurate butt joint.

1

2

POCKET HOLE SCREW JOINTS

Pocket hole screw joints offer a strong butt joint. This joint is used on the unexposed side of the joint, such as in face frames or even picture frames. An angled drilling jig and a special drill bit are needed to drill the pocket holes. Special flathead screws help pull the joint together.

1. The pocket hole drilling jig locks the board and allows the drill to bore the holes at an angle. Note the stop collar, which is set to drill to the proper depth.

2. Drilling the pocket hole screws home to make the solid butt joint.

(continued on page 56)

Joinery (continued)

Other than the butt joint, there are many other ways to join wood, including grooving, rabbets (see page 58), dados, and mortise and tenon. These joints can be made using a table saw or router. Here are some useful options to explore.

DADOS

The dado groove allows a board to be joined at 90 degrees to another board. The groove must be the same width as the joining board, which fits into it. The interlocking joint is then glued and clamped. Dado joinery is used to make bookshelves and other types of cabinet boxes called case work. Dado grooves are made with the table saw or the router.

A dado blade set is used to make grooves, dados, and rabbets on the table saw. These blades can be stacked to create any width groove from ¼" to ¹³⁄₁₆". Shims can be added to fine-tune the cuts.

1. To make a dado joint in ¾" panels, stack the dado blades to that dimension. Lower the blades to make a ⅜" deep cut in the panel. Notice the backer board attached to the miter fence. This will prevent tear out as the blades exit the back of the plywood. Tear out is when wood fibers are pulled out and not cleanly cut. This occurs when cutting across the grain.

BELOW, CENTER Cutting a dado.

BELOW, RIGHT The dado is a strong joint when glued up. This type of joint is used in making shelves and bookcases.

ABOVE A dado blade set

MITERS

Miter joints, in which the ends of the two pieces to be joined are each cut to 45 degrees and aligned, are ideal for joining corners at 90 degrees. This is a good-looking joint, but it needs some internal strengthening device such as a biscuit or spline to make a secure glue joint.

Biscuit slots are cut into each face of the miter using a biscuit slotting machine. Wooden, oval-shaped biscuits are glued and inserted into the slots. The biscuits swell with the moisture from the glue and ensure a tight joint. The spline joint is similar except a slot is cut at 90 degrees into the length of each miter face and is cut to fit into the slots, then glued and clamped.

The miter joint can also be strengthened using keys, ⅛" thick wooden wedges, glued into slots cut at 45 degrees to the corner. The end grain of a miter cut does not make a strong glue joint on its own. (More detailed instructions for making the miter joint is covered on page 68.)

MORTISE AND TENON

The mortise and tenon joint, in which an extended part of one piece (the tenon) is fitted into a corresponding notch (the mortise) in the other piece, is a strong way to hold a joint together. This joint is more difficult to make because one piece must fit into the other exactly, but it offers a lot of glue surface. A through mortise and tenon joint not only offers strength but adds a decorative touch to the joint. The mortise is cut all the way through the piece, leaving an open slot. The tenon is cut with an additional length to protrude through the mortise. A contrasting wedge is usually forced into a slot in the exposed tenon for added strength. The mortise and tenon joint is used to join table aprons to legs, large and small door frames, and supporting stretchers.

HALF-LAP JOINTS

Half-lap joints, in which the two joined pieces are cut so they overlap, hold frames together. The joint is strong because it has a large amount of glue surface area. This joint can be made using a set of dado blades raised to half the thickness of each board. Use a miter gauge to pass the wood over the dado blades to nibble away the wood to the proper length. Half-lap joints can also be made using the router table, or sawed by hand. Different width boards can be joined as long as they are the same thickness.

(continued on page 58)

Joinery (continued)

END RABBET

The end rabbet joint, in which the ends of two connecting boards nest into each other, makes a strong corner. This joint is used for making drawers, joining cabinet panels, and boxes. The end rabbet is cut on the table saw using dado blades. The end rabbet can be made using a rabbeting bit in a hand-held router or on the router table. The rabbeting bit has interchangeable bearings of different diameters to adjust the depth of cut.

1. To create the end rabbet joint in ¾" plywood, you can use the same dado blade set up. This time, however, you will cut a groove ⅜" × ⅜" on the end of each panel instead of a ¾" groove. A sacrificial fence is used to protect the table saw fence and it also covers half of the ¾" stack of blades. Set the fence to allow a ⅜" cut or half the thickness of the plywood.

2. The end rabbet joint allows for a lot of glue surface. This is a strong joint used for making drawers or cabinet joinery.

FRAME VERSUS CARCASE CONSTRUCTION

In frame construction, boards are joined using mortise and tenon, pocket hole, dowels, or biscuit techniques. Table aprons are joined with mortise and tenon to table legs. Frame and panel doors are examples of frame construction. Miter joints and lap joints connect frames. Through mortise and tenon exposing the wedged joint is a decorative way to join frames.

Carcase or case construction is when ends of boards are joined using tongue and groove, dovetails, or miters. End rabbets, finger joints, biscuit joints, and simple butt joints are common joints used in this type of joinery. These two major categories of joinery aren't mutually exclusive. Carcases are also joined with butt joints, rabbets, dados, grooves, pocket screws, dowels, and biscuits. Drawers, boxes, and cabinets are examples of carcase construction. Frames are sometimes mitered, lapped, joined with sliding dovetails, or tongue-and-groove joints as well.

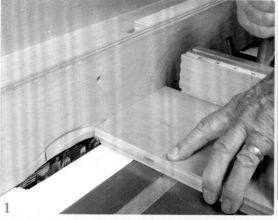

Hardware Basics

Selecting the proper screws, nails, hinges, knobs, handles, or drawer slides are all considerations to plan for and incorporate into your designs. You don't have to buy out the hardware store to have every type, size, or style of screw or nail on hand. When planning your project, always include the hardware specs you need to finish the job well.

When choosing screws, look for the proper length, size, and the type of driving recess at the top of the screw. There are many styles of screw drives available. Avoid the slotted head screw because it is difficult to drive, and the driver cannot be angled as it will slip out of the slot. The most widely used head style is the Phillips drive. Another popular drive innovation is the combo head, which has Phillips-type slots with a square hole in the center. The square drive head is used in pocket hole screws and other types of screws because it can take a lot of torque without slipping. Many of these screw types come in brass, stainless, coated, and painted.

The use of the traditional nail has changed with the innovation of power brad and pin nailers. These nailers are powered by air compressors. Brad nailers eliminate the need for a nail set to drive in finishing nail heads when installing molding or trim work the traditional way with a hammer. Pin nailers drive in fine pins hardly visible and work well with thin molding as they do not split the wood. Finishing nails, brads, and tacks still have their place in the wood shop and many traditionalists prefer to use them.

TIP Hardware Storage

A great way to keep track of your screws, nails, and other hardware is to purchase some clear plastic storage bins that can be mounted to a wall. Identify each drawer using self-adhesive labels. This way you can quickly see when you are running low on certain hardware.

Screw head styles and screwdrivers

A. The square drive screw is used in pocket hole applications and anywhere else high-torque screws are needed. It has a lot of contact surface and will not round out. Square drive sizes are coded 1, 2, and 3.

B. The combo head screw offers a Phillips and square drive all in one. This style offers a good grip and is used for cabinet making.

C. The Phillips drive screw is the most popular style. It's used in many different applications. They are less expensive than the other style of drives.

D. The square drive bit is used to drive the square drive screw. These bits come in many different lengths and the square sizes are numbered 1, 2, and 3.

E. The combo drive bit drives the combo style screws. This bit will not fit in a Phillips recess.

F. The Phillips driver bit comes in three sizes, 1, 2, and 3.

HINGES

Hinges can add that special touch to a box or door. They can also be hidden or concealed. Selecting cabinet and drawer hardware can be an all-day job. There are thousands of styles and materials to choose from.

Choosing Glue

Glue is used to secure most of these joints. It locks the joint and gives it longevity. A century ago, most of the glue used for furniture making was derived from extracts made from hides, hooves, and fish. In parts of Asia, glue was made from mashed boiled rice. Today hide glue is still used for certain applications, such as hammer veneering.

The glues available today are highly specialized and accommodate many types of applications. When selecting your glue, read the label closely for what types of materials or applications are recommended. Glue's open time (the time from when it is applied to when it starts to set up or harden) is critical, especially when doing intricate glue ups. The shelf life of glues should be checked. Old glue won't work and should be discarded.

There are many ways to apply glue. Special applicator bottles allow glue to be rolled onto a surface. Small brushes can be used to place glue into irregular shapes. Applying glue to large surfaces can be done with a small paint roller. Hypodermic syringes are used to place glue into tight places.

Here are some of the most commonly used types of glue to choose from.

PVA glue (yellow glue) is the standard for general woodworking. This glue has a longer working time, which allows you to glue all the joints together before it sets up. It cleans up with water. Care should be taken not to apply too much glue to the joints. Glue squeeze out occurs when clamps are tightened to hold the glued surfaces together. If there is too much glue applied to the joint it will ooze out of the clamped

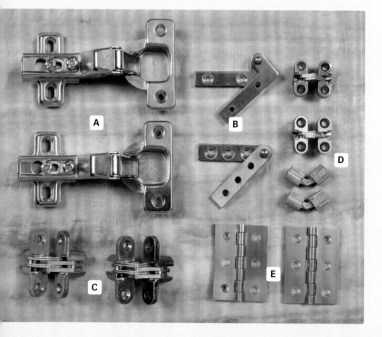

Hinges come in many different forms.

A. The Euro-style hinges are concealed hinges used on cabinet doors. They have a quick disconnect feature, to make it easier to remove the door, and three-way adjustments for precise door alignment. There are several configurations that offer inset, full overlay, or half overlay. They can be used on frameless or face frame cabinets.

B. Brass knife hinges must be mortised into the carcase and the door. The straight type is used for overlay doors while the offset L-hinge is for flush-mounted doors. These hinges make an elegant statement.

C. The large SOSS invisible hinges are recessed and they are ideal for a flush, smooth surface. They are used for light load bearing installations. They can open 180 degrees.

D. Miniature SOSS hinges are used for small boxes or lids. They mount flush and are hidden when in the closed position.

E. Solid brass cabinet hinges give an elegant, quality finish to any cabinet.

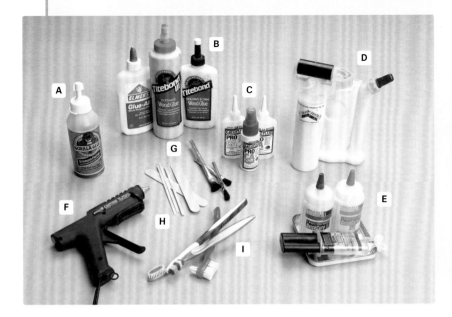

A sample of the variety of available glues.

A. polyurethane glue
B. white and yellow glues
C. cyanoacrylate glue (super glue)
D. roll-on and squeeze-type applicators
E. two-part epoxies
F. hot-melt glue gun
G. brushes used to apply glue
H. stick-type applicators
I. toothbrushes used to clean glue squeeze out

joint and is difficult to clean up. It can leave a residue that will show up when finish is applied. This type of glue should only be used for interior projects because it is not waterproof.

Contact cement is ideal for gluing on plastic laminates to substrate such as MDF or plywood. The cement should be applied to both surfaces and allowed to dry. Then the laminate can be placed onto the substrate for an instant bond. Use a roller to press out the surface. If you are gluing a large piece, dowels should be placed every 8" on the substrate after the glue dries. Then you can place the laminate on the dowels, which will keep the laminate from sticking while adjustments are made. The dowels can be removed one at a time so the laminate can slowly connect to the substrate.

Cyanoacrylate glue (super glue) sets quickly and is great for repairing small parts. It will bond wood to other materials. Wood turners use this glue to bond cracks and voids on their bowls and vessels.

Two-part epoxies don't shrink once they are dry and are waterproof. This type of glue is used in boat-building and outdoor furniture. Some of these products set up in five minutes, while other types have longer working times. Epoxy can be colored by adding dye to match the color of wood that is being repaired. Epoxy is ideal for permanent bonding of a threaded insert or T-nuts to wood.

Plastic resin glue is moisture resistant. This product comes in powder form and must be mixed with water. Wear a vapor-type mask while working with the powder, because it is toxic to breathe. This glue is used to make bent laminations (see page 86). It has a long open working time (about twenty minutes), which helps while clamping up or placing the form into a vacuum bag. It should stay clamped for eight hours for proper curing. It should set solidly to prevent creep and slippage.

Hot-melt glue is for a temporary hold. This type of bond can be used to hold templates and patterns to wood for routing. Care should be taken to remove any residue left by the glue. Some types of glue sticks set up quicker than others. See the directions on the package. This bonding method is used to connect corrugated, foam core, or plastic to make prototype models.

Polyurethane glues are tough and water resistant. This type of glue needs moisture to start the curing process. Apply the glue sparingly to one piece of wood; apply moisture using a damp sponge to the mating piece of wood. Clamp them up. In a few minutes foam will start to appear at the glue joint. Let this harden before removing. A sharp chisel can slice off the hardened foam. Polyurethane glue has a shorter working time but offers a strong, waterproof bond. Waterproof glue is a necessity for any project that will have outdoor use.

Hand-Cut Through Dovetails to Join a

WOOD PROJECT Shadow Box Frame

Your skills will be on display when you master cutting dovetails by hand. This elegant joint dates back to the ancient Egyptians. There are many types of dovetails but for this project you will be making through dovetails. This frame can be used to display a picture or it can be made deep enough to house a three-dimensional object. The frame can be hung or it can rest on a table.

TOOLS

- table saw
- jointer
- planer
- ruler
- square
- bevel gauge
- marking gauge
- marking knife
- dovetail saw
- bench chisels
- bench plane

PREPARING THE WOOD

1. Before you start cutting any dovetails, the wood has to be properly prepared. Here, black walnut is the wood of choice. If you have never cut dovetails by hand before, I suggest you start with a secondary wood such as poplar or maple. Whatever the species of wood you choose, it must be milled perfectly flat. You'll need 8" × 8' × ¾" poplar (or wood of your choice). Check to make sure the board is not warped, bowed, or cupped.

2. Using your table saw set the fence to 3" from the blade. Rip two strips lengthwise to this dimension. Using a table saw sled or a miter gauge, crosscut (cut across the grain or at 90 degrees) these strips to 25" long. This will give you plenty of pieces for practice. Check the flatness of these pieces again. The final thickness of this frame will be ⅝". You can now move these pieces to your jointer.

3. Make crisscross marks on the 3" wide side of your wooden strips with a pencil. Using a push stick, run the penciled side of the board over the planer blades. If all of the pencil marks are removed in this pass, you can be assured of a flat side. If not, repeat again. Repeat this for the rest of the boards.

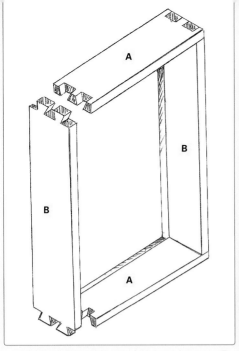

Use this diagram with the estimating template on page 67.

4. Now you want to surface one edge of each board. With the flattened side of the board against the fence set at 90 degrees, push the edge of the board over the jointer blades. This should assure you a square edge on one side of the board. Mark this edge with a pencil. Repeat this for all boards.

5. Now these boards can be planed to $^5/_8$". Place the flattened side down on the planer bed, and bring down the cutter head to start removing the wood. Plane no more than a $^1/_{16}$" in each pass. Watch your grain direction to eliminate any tear outs. If you detect any chipping, turn the piece around. When all the boards are surfaced to $^5/_8$", it is time to move to the table saw again.

6. Set the fence to the final dimension of $2^1/_2$" and lock it down. Place the board with the previously marked pencil edge against the fence. Set your blade about $^1/_8$" above the $^5/_8$" milled board. Using a push stick, rip all of the boards to the new dimension. Now these boards have to be cut to length, making sure each edge is square. This is achieved by setting your miter gauge to 90 degrees. Double-check this by using a square on the saw blade and a miter gauge. Make any adjustment and lock it down. At this point, screw a $^3/_4$" × 22" × 4" plywood backer to the miter gauge; let it extend at least 15" to the left. This backer

board will serve two purposes: It will support the piece being cut and will eliminate any tear out. Trim one side of each piece only. Clamp a stop block to the backer at a preset dimension to allow for accurate, repeatable cut-offs. Flip the pieces over and cut the opposite edge to the proper lengths. Now all the pieces should be flat, square, and ready to start practicing making dovetails.

When preparing boards for this project, they must be flat with no cupping or warping. It is essential that they all be the same thickness and the same width. This can be achieved using the jointer and planer. Each end must be truly square. The length of the two sides must be equal. The top and bottom must also be equal length.

TIP Inside or Outside?

Arrange the top and sides with the best grain showing on the outside. With chalk or marker on tape, mark a pyramid symbol pointing up on the outside of each board. This should eliminate any confusion when marking your pins and tails. You will always know where the inside and outside of the panels are.

(continued on page 64)

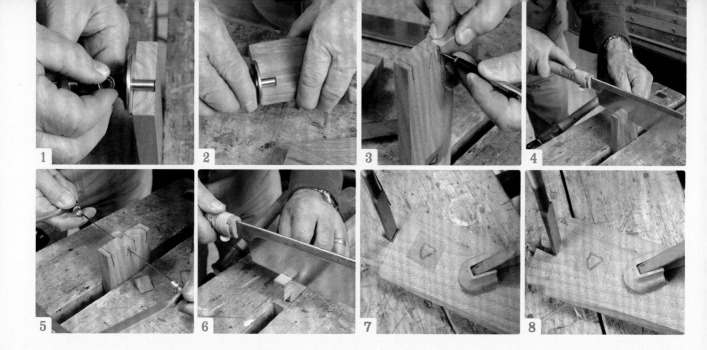

MARKING AND MEASURING YOUR DOVETAILS

Some people start marking out the pins first, others start with the tails. The tails are the wide, flat shapes that resemble the spread tail of a bird. The pin board has the narrow, tapered wedges that fit in between the tails. This exercise will start with the tails (left and right) pieces first.

1. Set your marking gauge to the thickness of the milled wood plus $\frac{1}{64}$".

2. Scribe both ends of all the boards on the front, back, and sides. Use tape on the outside of each board to indicate the top edge of the finished frame.

3. Use a bevel gauge or a commercially available dovetail template to mark out the tails. Keep the angle between 1:6 and 1:8. This angle is calculated by drawing a vertical line 8" long connected at the top to a 1" horizontal line forming half of a T. Now draw a line from the right side of the T down to the 8" mark. This angle is 1:8. If the angles are too steep the edge could crack off.

    Lay out the angles of the tails on the front of the piece. Use a square to carry these lines across the end grain edge. Continue the angled lines down the other side, stopping at the scribed line.

4. Using a dovetail saw, follow the marked lines. Carefully cut the tails down to the scribed line. Do not cut below the scribed line because these cuts will show up on the finished assembly. There are two types of dovetail saws. One is the Western style of saw, which cuts on the push stroke. Here, I use a Japanese saw, which cuts on the pull stroke. The pull saw has a thinner blade and delivers a thinner kerf. When cutting, angle the saw to match the angle of the marked line. Some people will angle the board in the vise and hold the saw vertically.

5. Use a scroll saw to cut out most of the waste. This will make paring with the chisels a lot easier.

6. Carefully cut to the scribed line when taking off the end pieces. Use your thumb against the side of the saw as a guide to start the cut.

7. Clamp the tail board securely. With a bench chisel, pare away the waste at a 10-degree angle. This will undercut the opening between the tail pieces. Make sure to use a chisel that is close to the same width as the opening between the tails. After cutting halfway through, flip the board over and continue the undercutting. Stay away from the scribed line until you have relieved the interior of the opening.

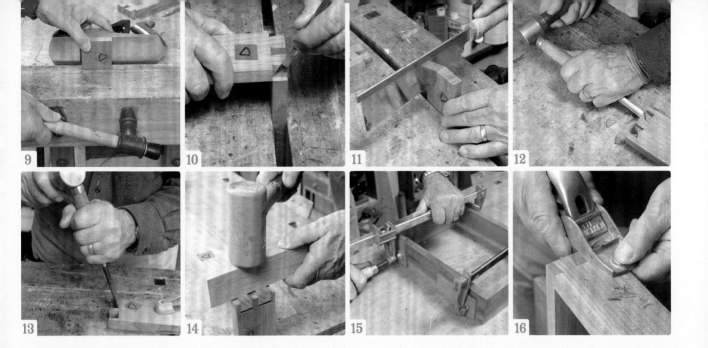

8. Now there should only be the scribed line remaining. Drag your chisel and let it click into the scribed line with the flat of the chisel facing inward. Tap the chisel down vertically to complete the cut. This should give you a flat, even edge between all of the tails.

9. To scribe the tails to the pins accurately, clamp the pin board in the vise flush to the side of a smoothing plane. This will set the pin board square to the top of the plane body.

10. Pull the plane away 5" and lay the tail board on top of the plane. Hold the tail board flush to the pin board and scribe the tails with a marking knife. Project the scribed lines on the tail board, using a square to mark verticals to the previous scribe depth lines.

11. Saw snugly to the inside of the line of the areas that are to be cut away. Mark the area to be eliminated so there are no mistakes. Again, carefully cut down to the horizontal scribed line.

12. Again, use your scroll saw to eliminate most of the wood between the pins. Now chisel out most of the waste holding the chisel horizontally. Stay away from the scribed lines.

13. Repeat the undercutting with the chisel (as was done on the tails, step 7). Make sure your final chop is on the scribed line. You may have to do some clean up and paring with your chisels to adjust the final fit of the joint. If the fit is too tight, rub some graphite or pencil on either the pins or tails and check the fit. This should reveal the area that is binding and needs to be trimmed. If you try to force the fit, the joint could split.

14. Dry-fit your joint before gluing. Check that it is square. If the fit is good, apply some yellow glue to the inside of the pins using a thin stick. Apply the glue sparingly to prevent any squeeze out. Use a dead blow hammer or a block of wood to tap the joint together.

15. Clamp the frame. Use wood pads next to the dovetails to apply pressure to the joint to ensure a tight fit. Check again for square. Set aside and let the glue dry for an hour.

16. Using a small, sharp block plane, carefully shave away any end grain protrusions. Always direct the plane into the frame to prevent tear out on the edges.

(continued on page 66)

1

2

3

MAKING A RABBET GROOVE INSIDE THE FRAME

To allow this frame to accommodate a picture and glass, a groove called a rabbet must be cut into the back. This is done with a rabbeting router bit in the router table.

1. Set the rabbeting bit so the blades are ⅜" above the bottom of the frame. The guide bearing will allow a shallow ⅛" cut. This cut can be made in one pass as it does not cut out a lot of wood. This will form the recess groove in the back of the frame.

2. Turn on your router. Place the inside of the frame snug against the bearing. Make sure you use push blocks for this operation to keep from accidentally trimming your nails (or your fingers). Push the frame from left to right, all the way around the inside surface. This is basically a shallow cut and should not produce tear out. Should you hear a ripping or cracking sound, this could be the warning of tear out. Move the frame away from the bit and turn off the router. Check the area for a change of grain direction. Lower the router bit and make a series of lighter cuts. You could also reverse the direction of the cut to get less tear out in the problem section.

3. This technique will give you a nice even rabbet to cradle your picture and glass.

SQUARING THE CORNERS

4. The rounded corners can now be squared off using your bench chisel. Use a square and a marking knife to scribe square corners. Do not try to chop down the full depth in one blow. Carefully cut down to the proper depth.

5. Install a chamfering bit with a rub bearing into your router table. Flip the frame over on its front and route from left to right. Make sure the chamfering bit is set to only relieve a ¼" of depth. This will ensure the front edge is not too thin.

6. This chamfer will give your frame a finished look. You could use other router profiles to dress up the frame. (For more on router bits, see page 102 in chapter 6.)

Hand Planing

The block plane is an essential hand tool for your arsenal. This small, versatile plane is used to soften edges, cut bevels, and trim work. Some block planes are designed with a low angle cutting. The blade is angled at 37 degrees so it requires less force when cutting through end grain. This keeps the blade from dulling quickly. The standard angle block plane has its blade set at 45 degrees. It cuts cleaner for long grain or horizontal cutting.

As with any cutting tool, the blade has to be sharp. The sole, or bottom of the plane, must be flat and free of any scratches or mill marks. Block plane blades cut with the bevel facing up. The larger bench and smoothing plane blades cut with the bevel facing down.

Some block planes have an adjustable sole to increase or decrease the throat opening. This is the opening between the blade and the sole. Decreasing the throat opening will produce fine shavings. Increasing the opening will make heavier cuts.

Wax the sole of your planes. This helps the plane glide smoothly over the work and protects against rust.

> **TIP** | **Filling in the Gaps**
>
> Sometimes there are small, poor-fitting gaps between the dovetail joints. To repair, make a mixture of shellac and sawdust from your wood. Force this mixture into the gap and let it dry. Sand and check for color match. If the gap is wide, use a thin sliver of the same wood that is oriented with the same grain direction and glue into the opening.

Estimating Template for:
Shadow Box Frame

			Rough Dimensions		Final Dimensions		Stock		Board Feet	Lumber Cost	Material Cost
Symbol	Part	Qty	Width	Length	Width	Length	Solid	Ply			
A	Top and bottom	2	3"	10"	2½"	9"	Walnut				
B	Sides	2	3"	13"	2½"	12"	Walnut				

Use this estimating template with the diagram on page 63.

Make a Presentation Box Using the
WOOD PROJECT Miter Joint

To make this elegant box, choice black walnut with a highly figured grain was selected to make the sides and ends. The top was made from spalted maple that was resawn or vertically cut in half, book-matched, and glued. The contrast of the dark walnut with the light maple gives this box some visual excitement. Contrasting maple wedges are inserted into the mitered corners. This gives both strength and decorative elements to the box.

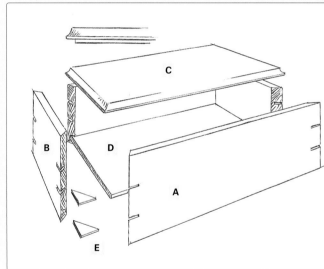

Use this diagram with the estimating template on page 71.

TOOLS

- table saw
- band saw
- miter saw
- edge clamps
- band clamps
- ruler
- bench plane
- router table
- flush-cut Japanese saw

BOX DIMENSIONS

The finished dimensions of the box are:

A. Side panels: 3" × 10" × ⅝"
B. End panels: 3" × 5' × ⅝"
C. Top: 5⅜" × 10⅜" × ½"
D. Bottom: 4³⁄₁₆" × 9½" × ⅛"
E. Wedges: ⅛" maple

Add 1' in length to the side and end panels. This will allow miters to be cut on each end to make the final trim size.

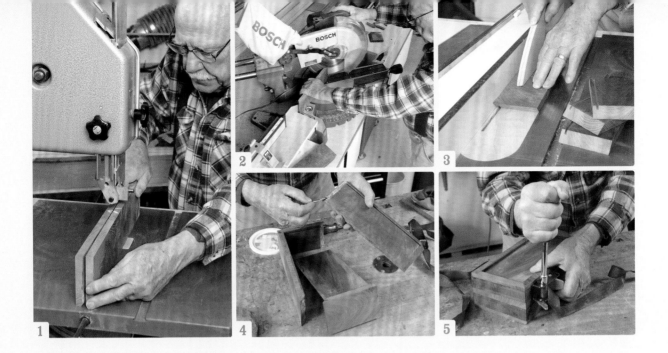

The bottom of the box was milled from scrap walnut down to ⅛" thick. This type of wood is sometimes considered junk because it is light sap wood; but it can easily be rescued from the woodpile for many applications. This thin milling process is described on page 39.

1. Resaw the highly figured walnut into ¾" planks on the band saw. Joint and plane these boards to ⅝" thick. Care should be taken while planing to check the grain direction. Highly figured wood is notorious for grain tear out. (See page 38 for more on preparing the wood.)

2. To create the mitered corner joints of the box, set your miter saw to 45 degrees and lock in. Cut some tests strips to make sure your miters are exact. Now cut your miters on only one end of the sides and ends. Make your length measurements from the mitered end you just cut. To ensure repeatability, use a stop block to cut the other end of each piece.

3. Cut grooves for the bottom. Set the table saw fence to ¼". Lower your blade to cut a ¼" high groove. Cut a groove in the inside base of each piece to receive the ⅛" thick bottom. After cutting these grooves it is essential that you sand the inside surfaces and the bottom before assembling. Shellac can be applied to the inside as long as none gets on the mitered corners that are to receive glue. Sand the shellacked surfaces with fine grit paper. This will save you a lot of grief from trying to do this after the box was glued together.

4. Mill and cut the bottom to size. Brush a thin coat of yellow glue on each of the mitered corners. Let the glue set on the mitered edges for two minutes; this will let the glue start to seep into the end grain. Slip the bottom into the grooves. Do not use any glue on the bottom. The bottom should float in the grooves. Make sure the box is resting on the table upside down. This will help to ensure the top edges will be flat.

5. Use band clamps on the top and the bottom of the box. This will draw the mitered corners together for a good tight fit. Any glue squeeze out on the inside corners can be scooped out using a straw that has been cut on an angle. A dampened toothbrush will also help clean out glue in the corners.

(continued on page 70)

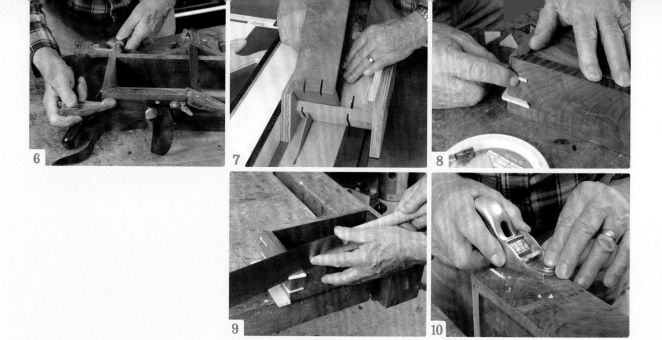

6. Flip the box over on its bottom and check the top edges to make sure they are flush. Use bench clamps to help draw the miters closer together if needed.

7. Glue joints on end grain do not offer the strongest joint, because there is a small amount of surface area and no long grain to adhere to. To strengthen the mitered joint, insert decorative wedges. Using a sled on the table saw allows you to accurately cut slots on the mitered corners to receive these wedges. Guide the sled against the fence. Flip the box over on each corner to receive the slots.

Make sure the blade is not set too high as it may protrude through the inside of the box.

The sled is basically a 90-degree corner made of ¾" MDF that is glued between two pieces of ¾" plywood at 45 degrees. This supports the piece being slotted. The sled rides against the fence. Raise the blade of the saw high enough to cut a slot through the MDF and into the corner of the box.

8. Cut your wedges from ⅛"-thick maple stock, apply glue, and insert into the cut slots. This will allow for good edge-to-edge glue surfaces. Put aside and let the glue dry. (See page 39 for more on milling thin wood.)

9. Using a Japanese flush-cutting saw, carefully shear off the protruding wedges. Japanese saws cut on the pull stroke. Start cutting from the corner as not to tear out the tip of the wedge. I prefer the Japanese-style saw because there is no set on the teeth. This eliminates marring or scratching the surface. The saw is very flexible and allows cutting in tight places.

10. Using a small sharp block plane trim the wedges flush to the sides. Always trim in from the corner so the tips of the wedges are not sheared off. Now you can sand the outside and get it ready for the finish.

TIP   Book Match

"Book match" is used to describe a plank of wood that is vertically cut in half or resawn and opened like a book. This reveals a matching grain pattern on the left and right panels. The facing edges are then jointed straight and square. These two edges are glued and clamped together. After the glue dries the panel is put through the planer to even out the surfaces.

11
12
13

11. Cut the book-matched lid to size. Install a ½" cove bit in the router table. This will give you a concave edge. Set the bit to protrude ⅛". Place the lid with the face down. Start with the end grain side to make the first cut. Using a miter gauge, push the lid through the cove bit. Cut the other end grain side. If there is any tear out on the end grain edge, this should be healed while routing the long-grain side.

12. Now raise the bit another ⅛" and repeat the same process. There will now be a ¼" deep cove all around the lid. This exposes the end grain to frame this exciting piece of maple.

13. Going back to the table saw, install a ⅝"-wide dado blade set. Lower it to make a ⅛" deep rabbet. Use a sacrificial fence to protect the blades while cutting a ⁹⁄₁₆" wide rabbet underneath the lid to fit into the top of the box. A sacrificial fence is used to protect the table saw fence from being damaged by the saw blade. It could be as simple as a piece of ¾" × 4" plywood clamped to the fence to protect it from the dado blades while cutting the lip under the box lid.

 Note on Prefinishing

Using a finish (such as shellac) on the inside of boxes and drawers leaves an odorless finish. Oil and varnish tend to leave a long-lasting odor in an enclosed area. Another reason to prefinish the inside before glue up is to prevent any glue squeeze out from sticking to the finished surface.

Estimating Template for:
Presentation Box

Symbol	Part	Qty	Rough Dimensions Width	Rough Dimensions Length	Final Dimensions Width	Final Dimensions Length	Stock Solid	Ply	Board Feet	Lumber Cost	Material Cost
A	Sides	2	3"	12"	3"	10"	Walnut				
B	Ends	2	3"	6"	3"	5"	Walnut				
C	Top	1	6"	12"	5⅜"	10⅜"	½" Maple				
D	Bottom	1	5"	10"	4³⁄₁₆"	9½"	⅛"Walnut				
E	Wedges	8					⅛" Maple				

Use this estimating template with the diagram on page 68.

Hanging Euro-Style
WOOD PROJECT Wall Cabinet

The techniques used in making this cabinet can be applied to any size hanging cabinet that may be needed in the kitchen, bathroom, or any other location. The cabinet is made of ¾" oak plywood. Two techniques are used to hide the plywood edges: Iron-on veneer strips and solid oak edging that is biscuit-joined to the exposed plywood edge.

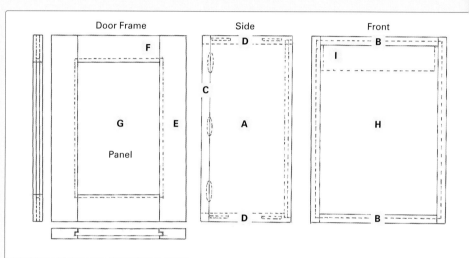

Use this diagram with the estimating template on page 77.

TOOLS

- table saw with sliding miter gauge
- biscuit slotting machine
- router table
- engineer's squares
- drill press
- Forstner bit

- clamps
- pin hole gauge
- electric drill
- sanding machine
- bench plane
- file
- electric iron

There are many joinery techniques used in making this little cabinet. The flush overlay door is attached by using European-style hinges. The interior of the cabinet is drilled for shelf pin holes. These allow the shelf to be adjusted. The cabinet will be mounted to the wall using a French cleat. The cabinet case is joined using glue and biscuits. The panel door uses tongue-and-groove joinery.

It is wise to prepare a cut list to keep track of all the parts that are needed. The cut list is used when ordering lumber and sheet goods. After you have drawn your plans, assign each part a number or letter. See page 48 for more about creating cut lists for your projects.

Lay out the sides, top, and bottom on your plywood. Cut these to size and prepare to apply the edge banding to the top and bottom of the sides. The solid oak facings are biscuited to the front of these four pieces.

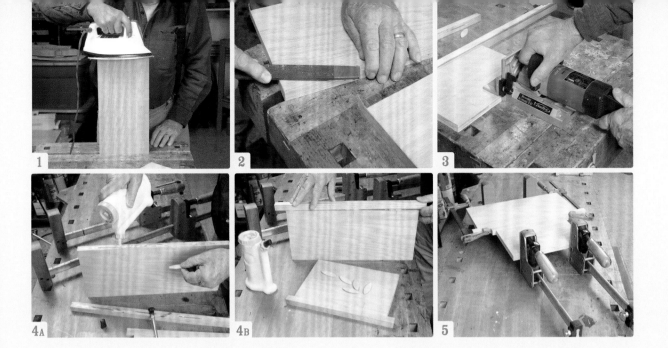

1. Apply iron-on edge banding veneer to the top and bottom of each side. Make sure the iron is hot enough to melt and seal the banding to the plywood edge. The banding should be cut longer than the width of the board. These overhangs can be trimmed later.

2. Use a file held at a slight angle to remove the overhang of the edge banding. Tape the end of your file to keep from marring the plywood. Always file one way into the board in order to prevent pulling the banding up from the edge of the plywood. Snap off the overhanging ends and again file into the edge. Be careful not to file away the edge of the veneer surface on the plywood.

3. Cut the ¾" by ¾" solid oak facings a little longer than the length of the plywood you are attaching them to. Place the oak facings against the side of the plywood they will be attached to. Mark a pencil line across the plywood and oak facing to indicate where the biscuit slots will be cut. Mark an arrow on the oak facing to indicate what side to cut the slots. The slots should be placed about 8" to 10" apart. Biscuits come in several sizes; #10 and #20 are the most common. Number 20 will be used for this project. Biscuit-slot the oak facings and the plywood and prepare to glue them up.

The biscuit cutting machine has adjustments to set the cutting depth of the blade to match the biscuit size. There is a depth adjustment to set the slot cut to match the thickness of the wood being grooved. Some machines have an adjustable fence to set any angle from 0 to 90 degrees.

4. Apply glue to the biscuit slots on the plywood as well as the oak strips. Use a brush to even out the glue on the surfaces of each piece. Too much glue applied to the surfaces will wind up as squeeze out. Having to remove the excess glue will become a problem later.

Install the biscuits into the slots on the plywood edge and then put the banding on. Work quickly before the glue sets up. It is difficult to make any adjustments after the glue is hard.

5. To save time, glue and clamp up two panels at once. Make sure the oak facings are tight against the edges of the plywood. Any gaps here will show up when the carcase is assembled. Check for any glue that has squeezed out and scrape it off when the glue is still rubbery. Wiping off the wet glue with a wet cloth only smears the glue into the grain. This will create a problem when finishing. These pieces should remain in the clamps for at least two hours to assure good bonding.

(continued on page 74)

6. Most plywood today is less than ¾" thick. The ¾" oak strip will overhang the plywood about ¹⁄₆₄". This is where you must carefully plane the wood. Pencil marks on the plywood will notify you when the oak is flush with the plywood. When the pencil marks start to disappear, it is time to stop planing.

    This overhang can be trimmed using a router with a flush trimming bit. The router base is run on the narrow edges of the wood, so care should be taken not to rock the router. You can solve this problem by clamping a wide board flush to the top surface. This will support the router base.

7. Carefully trim off the oak extensions flush to the panels. This can be achieved by using the miter gauge on the table saw set at 90 degrees. Be careful not to cut into the veneer banding on the edge of the board. These surfaces should be flush.

8. Make your biscuit slots to the inside of your side panels. Do this both on the top and bottom of each of the side panels.

9. Biscuit slot the left and right ends of the top and bottom panels. Support these panels while slotting using bench dogs to push against them.

10. Drill four shelf pin holes on the inside of the left and right panels. This is a special hole-drilling jig made by Rockler to drill ¼" holes that will align perfectly.

11. Before assembly, it is wise to sand all inside surfaces. This would be a difficult chore to do after the carcase is glued together.

12. Apply glue and biscuits to the mating surfaces of the joints and start clamping the carcase. Check for a square and tight fit. Make sure the top and bottom panels are flush to the side panels. Any glue squeeze out on the interior corners can be eliminated by using water and a toothbrush. Another way to eliminate glue squeeze out on the inside is to use a drinking straw to scoop out any glue.

13. After the glue has dried and the clamps are off, it is time to cut the rabbet in the rear to receive the back panel and the French cleat. Install the rabbeting bit into the router table and cut a ¾"-deep rabbet. Remember to always move clockwise when routing on the inside of the carcase. The ¾"-deep rabbet will allow for the ¼" back and the ½"-thick French cleat.

14. With the back rabbeted, use your bench chisel to square up the inside corners. Notice that the back of the plywood is exposed. No banding was used as the back is against the wall.

15. Book-match and glue up the spalted maple to prepare for the door panel. Make sure the edges that will be glued are flat and even. After the glue dries this panel can be put through the planer to achieve the proper thickness. Again, watch grain direction to eliminate tear out. Use a light cut.

16. Measure and cut rails and stiles to the proper length for the door. Stiles are the vertical members of the door. Rails are the horizontal members. The rails and stiles of the door shown here are made of ¾" × 2¼" solid oak. When measuring the rails, add ¾" extra to provide for the ⅜" tongues on each end of the rail.

17. To make a tongue-and-groove joint, for this door, use dado blades to cut a ¼" × ⅜" deep groove on both the styles and rails. Set the fence on the table saw to cut to the center of ¾" wide wood. Make one cut, then flip the wood and make another pass. This will assure a groove that is centered on the styles and rails. These grooves may be a bit wider than ¼" but will be accounted for when cutting the tongues.

Another method to groove the rails and stiles would be to cut them on the router table. A ¼" slotting bit with a guide bearing is used for this operation. Adjust the height of the bit to be centered on the ¾" thick members. Use the proper diameter bearing to allow a ⅜" deep cut. Adjust the fence to be aligned with the bearing surface. You can now run the rails and stiles against the fence to cut the groove. Flip the boards over and run them through again. This will center the slots on the rails and stiles.

18. Cut the tongues on the ends of the rails to fit into the grooves made on the stiles. The depth of the tongues should match the depth of the grooves or ⅜". With the ¼" dado blades still in the saw, set the fence away from the blades by ⅛" and lock the fence. This should cut a ⅜" shoulder on the end of the rail. Set the height of the dado blades to cut away the wood to create the thickness of the tongue. This should be done on a test strip until the proper adjustments have been made. Use the sliding miter gauge set at 90 degrees to push the rail through the dado blades. After the shoulder cuts are made, you can move the rail back to nibble off the wood left on the end of the tongue.

(continued on page 76)

19. Before assembling the door, measure to install the Euro hinges. Use a square to pencil in the center lines from the right-hand door stile to the carcase.

20. Install a 35-mm Forstner drill bit into the drill press. Set the fence on the drill press table to position the drill bit ⅛" from the edge of the style. Drill the holes ½" deep to receive the hinge cups. Be sure to check the instructions that come with your hinges before you begin drilling. Some manufacturers use different dimensions for their products.

21. Place the hinges and screw them to the door stile and the carcase. Check the fit and action of the door on its hinges, then remove the hinges to allow for gluing up the door.

22. Before assembling the door, sand the inside of the rails and styles. This cannot be done after the glue up. Glue the bottom rail to the stiles and drop in the panel. Cut the panel and rabbet to fit the door frame. Sand and apply finish, but do not glue the panel to the door frame. This will allow the panel to float in the door frame.

23. After inserting the panel, apply glue to the top rail and insert into the frame. This completes the assembly of the door.

24. Check all alignment, and then apply clamps. Set aside to let the glue dry.

25. Fit and cut the back from ¼" plywood. Insert it into the back rabbet. Sand and apply finish to the inside of the back. Glue and brad nail to the carcase.

26. Make the French cleat. The French cleat allows you to hang the cabinet flush to the wall without drilling through the back of the cabinet. Using secondary wood such as pine or poplar, mill the cleat to ½" thick. The width should be 3". Set the blade on the table saw to 45 degrees. This table saw has a tilt to the right, which can be dangerous when using the fence on the right-hand side. Move the fence to the left of the 45-degree tilted blade to achieve the cut for the French cleat. The cut should divide the cleat in half.

27

28

27. Glue the top of the French cleat to the back and top of the cabinet with the bevel facing in and down. Screw the other half of the cleat to the wall with the bevel facing up and to the wall. This allows a nice flush fit.

28. Cut a shelf that is ⅛" narrower than the inside dimension of the carcase. Use ½" plywood and iron on the oak veneer to the front of the shelf and trim. It's ready for finishing.

Estimating Template for: Hanging Euro-Style Wall Cabinet

Symbol	Part	Qty	Rough Dimensions Width	Rough Dimensions Length	Final Dimensions Width	Final Dimensions Length	Stock Solid	Stock Ply	Board Feet	Lumber Cost	Material Cost
A	Sides	2			7¼"	16¼"		¾" Oak			
B	Top & bottom	2			7¼"	10⁹⁄₁₆"		¾" Oak			
C	Side facing	2			¾" × ¾"	17"	Oak				
D	Top & bottom facing	2			¾" × ¾"	12"	Oak				
E	Door stiles	2			2¼" × ¾"	16"	Oak				
F	Door rails	2			2¼" × ¾"	8¼"	Oak				
G	Front panel	1			7¾" × ¾"	12"	Maple				
H	Back	1			11"	5"		¼" Oak			
I	French cleat	1			2½" × ¾"	10½"	Oak				

Use this estimating template with the diagram on page 72.

Shaker-Style End Table with a Drawer

The Shaker style of furniture is a perennial favorite. The simplicity of its design allows it to blend with many other styles. This small end table is an example of typical Shaker construction. The legs and aprons are made from maple. The top is a combination of solid oak and oak plywood. The drawer is dovetailed and grooved to slide on runners that are attached to the aprons. This project is a little more complicated than the previous projects. It is advisable to have a cut list and to make full-size plans to double check your measurements while cutting the many pieces used in this project. The whole shop will be used for this project.

TOOLS

- table saw
- jointer
- planer
- router table
- biscuit slot cutter
- electric screwdriver
- hand clamps
- band clamps
- bench clamps
- drill press
- Forstner bits
- hollow chisel mortiser
- marking gauge
- tenoning jig
- taper cutting sled
- bench chisels

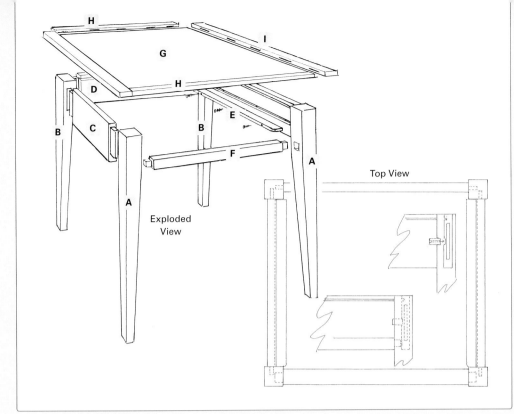

H

I

G

H

D

B

C

B

E

A

A

F

A

Exploded
View

Top View

The legs for this table are
tapered on two sides. Each
leg has mortises cut into
them to receive the tenons
on the ends of the aprons.

Use this diagram with the estimating template on page 85.

MAKING LEGS WITH A TAPER

1. Cut and mill the blanks for the legs to measure
   1⅝" square by 22" long. Group them together as
   they would appear on the finished table. Make
   witness marks on each pair and lay out the tapers to eliminate confusion and mistakes. The
   tapers should start 5" from the top of the leg and
   taper down to 1" square at the bottom.

2. Mark out the orientation for the mortises on the
   tops of the legs while they are clamped together.
   Indicate right rear, right front, left rear, and left
   front. You will refer to these many times during
   construction.

3. Carefully mark and scribe the areas to cut the
   mortises using a marking gauge. The top of the
   mortises should be ¾" down from the tops of
   the legs. The mortises for the back and side of
   the legs are all ¼" wide and 3" high and ¾" deep.
   These mortises will receive the side and back tenons of the aprons that are ¾" thick and 4½" deep.
   The side aprons are 15½" long, while the back
   apron is 17½" long. The mortises are set back to

allow a ¼" reveal on the legs. The mortises should
all be cut before the legs are tapered. This will
give a long stable surface while cutting mortises.

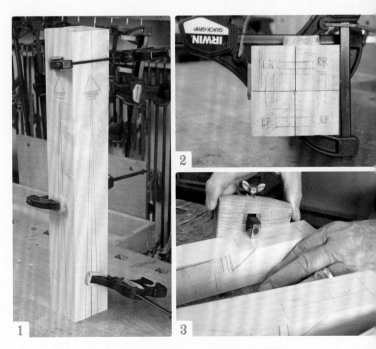

(continued on page 80)

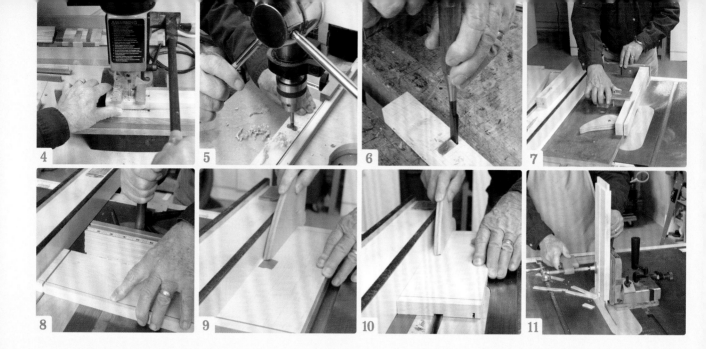

4. Install a ¼" mortising bit into the hollow chisel mortising machine. Set the depth to cut ¾" deep. Drill out the mortise to the scribed marks made earlier on the side and back legs. Mortises can also be made by drilling out the scribed area using a drill press with a ¼" Forstner bit. The mortise then can be cleaned up using a flat bench chisel.

5. Cut the mortises for the front stretcher that is 1" × 1½" into the left and right front legs. This mortise will be ½" × ¾" × ¾" deep. This can be done using a ½" Forstner bit in the drill press.

6. Square up the corners using a ½" bench chisel. With all the mortises cut, it is time to cut the tapers on the legs.

7. This simple, adjustable jig allows you to cut the tapers on the legs. The cam on the front of the jig lets you adjust the width of the taper. The clamping block in the center holds the leg in place. There is an adjustable back stop to adjust to the width of the leg blank. A runner fixed to the bottom of the jig rides in the track on the table saw. Cut the first taper, flip the leg over, and cut the second taper. Check the orientation that was marked on the leg earlier. This simple jig tracks parallel to the saw blade while the leg blank is clamped at an angle to achieve the taper.

8. Set the fence on the table saw to ⅝" to cut the shoulders for the side and back tenons to ¾". Use the miter jig to guide each apron.

9. Set the fence to ⅜" and the blade height to ⅜" and cut the grooves on the top inside faces of the side and back aprons. This groove will receive the tabletop cleats.

10. Set the fence to 2". Install dado blades to cut ½"-wide grooves, ⅛" deep. These grooves will house the drawer runners on the two side aprons.

11. Using a tennoning joint, cut the tenon cheeks on each side, leaving a ¼"-thick tenon using the tenoning jig on the table saw. This will be done to the side and back aprons.

12. Using the same setup, cut the cheeks for the tenons on the front stretcher. The tenons should be ½" wide.

13. Set the blade height to ¼" and cut away both sides of the tenon to wind up with a ½" × 1" tenon.

14. Set the saw blade to ¾" high and cut the top and bottom of each apron tenon. Cut off the top pieces with a hand saw.

15. Cut the ⅞" × ½" drawer runners to 14" long. This allows the runners to fit snugly between the front and back legs. Drill three countersunk holes using a drill with a chamfer collar attached or use a countersink bit after the hole is drilled. Round over the leading edge.

16. Lay out all the pieces on the full size plan and double check the measurements. Everything is now ready for a dry fit. If the tenons are too tight, use a shoulder plane or chisel to relieve some wood. Look for a snug fit, but be careful not to take too much wood away and allow the joint to be loose and wobbly. Make sure all of the aprons are flush with the tops of the legs.

17. Now the drawer runners can be screwed to the grooves in the side aprons. Make sure the rounded corners face forward. To enable the drawer to slide easily, smooth the edges of the runners with sandpaper.

18. The table is glued and clamped and is now ready to measure and fit the drawer.

(continued on page 82)

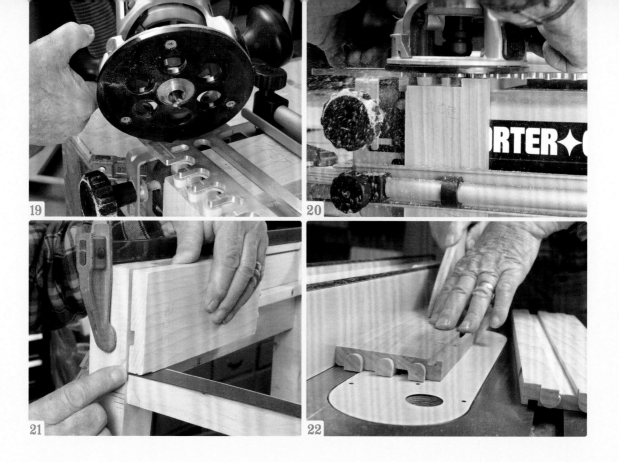

MAKING THE DRAWER USING MACHINE-CUT DOVETAILS

The drawer sides, front, and back are all milled to ⅝" thick and cut to 3½" wide. The boards must be flat with no bow or warp. Measure the drawer width between the front legs. Subtract ⅛" from this dimension to allow for a snug reveal. Measure the length of the drawer sides. Allow for the thickness of the front and back panels. Half-blind dovetails, which are not seen from the front of the piece, will be used to make this drawer. Cut the drawer panels to length making sure all edges are square. Make an extra panel or two to do test fits for the dovetails. Mark all the boards with witness marks to show the top and outside of each panel. Refer to the dovetail jig manufacturer for proper board orientation for routing dovetails on their jig.

19. The router base plate has a rub collar to follow the template on top of the jig. A dovetail bit rotates inside of the collar. This set up will cut half-blind dovetails on the front and side panels at the same time. Some adjustments may have to be made using the test panels to get a perfect fit.

20. Once the fit is perfect, this system will produce half-blind dovetails quickly. This set up is ideal for producing multiple drawers. (For more on routing dovetails, see page 113.)

21. Dado the ½" groove on the drawer side to ride on the guide rail. Make test fits using the extra panel pieces. Check the bottom reveal using a strip of laminate as a spacer. The width of the drawer panels may have to be trimmed.

22. Proceed to dado the grooves on the drawer sides to ride on the runners.

23. Dry-assemble the drawer and check for fit. The drawer should glide smoothly without any binding. The inside surfaces of the drawer should be sanded before assembly.

24. Assemble the drawer and secure with a band clamp. Check for square but do not glue up yet. Put a ¼" groove-cutting router bit in the router table. Cut the slot around the base of the drawer to receive the bottom. Guide the drawer clockwise.

25. Remove the back drawer panel and trim off the bottom to eliminate the strip where the groove was cut on the router table. This will allow the bottom to slide in after the drawer has been glued up. Glue the drawer front, back, and sides together, checking the assembly for square before the glue cures. Not a lot of glue is needed for these dovetails. Apply the glue sparingly using a small flux brush.

26. Measure and cut the drawer bottom from ¼" plywood. Drop it in and secure by screwing it to the bottom of the back drawer panel.

(continued on page 84)

MAKING THE TABLETOP

The top will be cut from ¾" plywood and surrounded by solid oak edge banding. Cut the front and back oak strips to ¾" square. These will be glued to the front and back of the oak plywood panel using biscuits. The oak strips should overhang the plywood to allow for flush trimming on the table saw.

27. Place a cross-cutting sled on the table saw. Put the plywood panel with the glued-up oak strips on the sled and trim each side to size.

28. Cut two ¾" thick solid oak strips to 2" wide and a little longer than the top. These will be faux breadboard edges. Draw register marks on the plywood and the oak strips to guide for cutting the biscuit slots.

29. Cut the biscuit slots into the plywood and the oak strips.

30. Glue and clamp the faux breadboard edges to the plywood top and put aside to dry.

31. Trim off the oak overhangs flush to the front and back of the top.

32. The ¾" solid oak edge banding is a bit proud of the plywood top. These can be carefully planed down to be flush with the plywood. When the pencil marks on the plywood start to disappear, it's time to stop. Give the top a light sanding to clean up any marks. Refer to chapter 9 for the finishing techniques used for this table.

33. Put the tabletop upside down and place the base on the tabletop, making sure it is centered. Insert the metal cleats into the slots in the aprons and secure with screws.

Breadboard Edges

The term breadboard edges stems from a joinery method used when tabletops and breadboards were made using solid wood boards glued together. These boards could cup, warp, expand, and contract due to heat and humidity. The exposed end grain edges would split and crack, leaving an ugly top. This problem was solved by making a tenon on the end of these boards and grooving an end board to cover the tenon. The breadboard was secured by a dowel embedded through the center of the breadboard and into the tenon. Two other dowels were drilled near each and of the breadboard. Where the dowels went through the tenon, it was slotted to allow for movement. Now the tabletop boards could move from the center out but were contained by the breadboard edge. This healed the ends of the table and gave it a nice finished feel.

Estimating Template for: Shaker-style End Table

Symbol	Part	Qty	Rough Dimensions Width	Length	Final Dimensions Width	Length	Stock Solid	Ply	Board Feet	Lumber Cost	Material Cost
A	Front legs	2	1¾" × 1¾"	24"	1⅝" × 1⅝"	22"	Maple				
B	Back legs	2	1¾" × 1¾"	24"	1⅝" × 1⅝"	22"	Maple				
C	Side aprons	2	5" × 1"	16"	4½" × ¾"	5½"	Maple				
D	Rear apron	1	5" × 1"	18"	4½" × ¾"	17½"	Maple				
E	Drawer runners	2			½" × ⅞"	14"	Maple				
F	Front stretcher	1	1¾" × 1¾"	18"	1½" × 1"	17½"	Maple				
G	Top	1			19"	17"		¾" Oak			
H	Front & back edge	2			¾" × ¾"	21"	Oak				
I	Breadboard edge	2			2"	21"	Oak				
J	Drawer sides	2			3⅜" × ⅝"	15"	Poplar				
K	Drawer front	1			3⅜" × ⅝"	15¾"	Poplar				
L	Drawer back	1			3" × ⅝"	15¾"	Poplar				
M	Drawer bottom	1			14¾"	15⅛"		¼" Oak			

Use this estimating template with the diagram on page 79.

BELOW Laminated wood can be formed into many shapes.

Bending
Laminated Wood

The fibers in wood grow straight and strong. When humans first tried to bend them, the fibers snapped, cracked, or splintered. Over the centuries, however, we have learned to coax wood to bend in many ways. Early artisans found that if they wet wood, it became pliable. If they steamed the wood, it could be bent onto forms, and once the wood dried it would maintain the shape of the form. Steam-bending techniques are still used in boat building and chair- and furniture-making.

Thin strips of wood can be bent with applied heat. This method uses the flame from a propane torch applied to a metal tube over which $\frac{1}{16}$"- or $\frac{1}{8}$"-thick wood strips are shaped. Wood formed in this manner is used for musical instruments, handles, and many other decorative purposes.

Thin strips of wood that are glued together are called laminations. The thicknesses of the wood strips vary according to the severity and thickness of the shape. The tighter the arc of the bend, the more chance there is of cracking or splitting the strips of wood. It is easy to test whether the strips are the right size before they are glued. If the strip cracks while bending, it has to be thinner. The sharper the bend, the thinner the laminations need to be to negotiate the curve. Check for knots or uneven grain as well, because these areas can cause a problem.

Wood species and grain direction also play an important role in the shaping process. Hardwoods such as cherry, walnut, ash, and maple are good choices for bent laminations because of their consistent grains. Ideally the grain direction should be parallel to the bend. Air-dried wood is best for bending because it is not as brittle as kiln-dried wood.

Laminate bending is strong because the grain direction follows the curve. The same shape could be cut from solid wood, but the grain direction would change around a curve and the resulting weak area could easily break. You would also waste a lot of wood.

Laminate bending offers more versatility than steam bending because you can mix species or alternate colors to create unique pieces.

Overview of the Lamination Process

When laminating, first apply glue to the wood strips. Then assemble them, place them into the form, and clamp in place so the glue can dry. This technique is versatile and can be used to form large architectural shapes such as curved panels and railings. Laminated wood is used in making contemporary furniture and delicate wood jewelry.

Vacuum-Bag Laminating Technique

Laminated strips are glued and placed over a curved MDF form in the vacuum bag. The pump extracts the air and the bag conforms to the shape.

Laminations can also be formed using the vacuum bag technique. Glued strips of wood are put on a form and placed into a plastic bag. The bag is sealed and a tube connected to a vacuum pump evacuates the air. The bag is sucked down and applies pressure to the lamination on the form. A pressure of 15 psi (pounds per square inch) holds the bag tight against the form for a long period of time while the glue dries. Irregular shapes and compound curves can be easily formed in this manner. Much of today's veneer work is done using the vacuum system because it eliminates clamping and two-part forms.

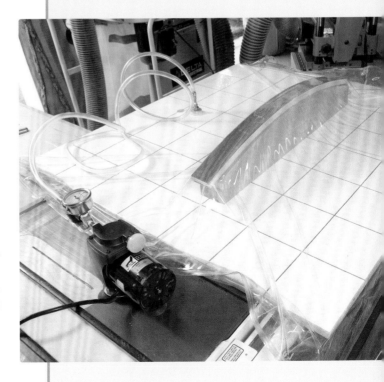

Laminated Wood
WOOD PROJECT **Salad Tongs**

This project was introduced to me twenty years ago by Tage Frid, a famous master woodworker and teacher. The tongs are an easy first lamination project, and they make great gifts. Once the form is made, it will last through hundreds of tong glue-ups. The form-making technique here can be applied to other shaped forms.

TOOLS

- table saw
- band saw
- block plane
- thickness planer
- screwdriver
- polyurethane glue
- two-sided carpet tape
- hand clamps

BUILDING THE FORM

Most forms are made of either plywood or MDF (medium-density fiberboard). When making forms with plywood, use Baltic birch because it does not have voids between layers and is much stronger. Use ¾" plywood to make this form. MDF is less expensive than plywood and is easy to machine. It would work just as well for making this form. Making this small form is a great way to use up those scraps of plywood or MDF hanging around in the cut-off bin.

1. Cut five pieces of plywood 3¾" × 13¼" . Glue these pieces with yellow glue then clamp and leave to dry for three hours.

2. Clean up any glue squeeze-out with a scraper. Trim to 3½" × 13" using the table or band saw.

3. Draw a wave-shaped curve on one of the faces of the blank freehand or with a French curve. This will be your guide for cutting the blank on the band saw.

(continued on page 90)

4. Make sure you have a sharp blade in your band saw. Cut slowly with a continuous motion to follow your drawn curve. Any ragged surfaces should be smoothed out by sanding. The smoother these two mating contours are, the smoother your lamination will be.

5. To ensure proper alignment, or registration, of the two halves of the form, glue and screw a cleat to each half to help align the form while clamping. Apply several coats of shellac or polyurethane finish to the form. This will keep any glue that squeezes out from sticking to the surface.

PREPARING WOOD FOR LAMINATIONS

It is preferable to use hardwoods such as oak, cherry, maple, or ash. You will need to prepare two pieces of wood 16" long, 3" wide, and ³/₆₄" thick. This can be achieved several ways.

• Start with a ¾"-thick stock cut to 3" wide. Using the band saw, cut the board in half to ³/₈" thick. This is called resawing, which is nothing more than cutting the wood horizontal to any desired thickness.

• You can also do this on the 10" table saw. Lower the saw blade to 1¼" above the tabletop. Set the fence to ³/₈" and rip the board in half then flip the board with the same side to the fence and rip the other half. Make sure you use a safe push block to do this. The thin rib that is left in the center can easily be separated on the band saw or by a hand saw.

If each board is thinner or thicker than ³/₈", this is no problem as they will be milled to ³/₆₄" in the planer. Most planers will not mill under a quarter inch. To get around this problem place the strips on a ½" or ¾" piece of plywood that is a little longer and wider than the strips. Secure the strips on the plywood with two-sided carpet tape and send them through the planer. You can now mill your two strips to ³/₆₄" in the planer.

6. Set the fence to ³/₈" and rip the ¾" board with blade height up to 1¼" and cut the first groove using a push block.

7. Flip your board and cut the second groove.

8. This rib allows for a safer cut on the table saw.

9. Move to the band saw and cut the rib.

10. Plane the boards to ³/₆₄" thick.

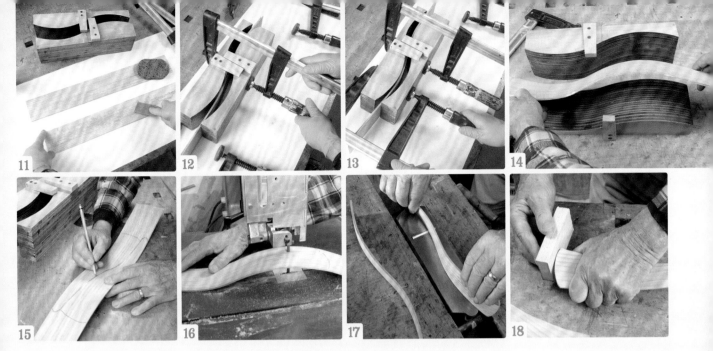

As you prepare to glue the pieces together, be sure to have clamps ready to compress your form on the laminate strips. Because these salad tongs will be used in a damp environment (dressed greens at the dinner table) and they will be washed frequently, use waterproof polyurethane glue. Wear vinyl gloves, because this glue can stain your fingers.

11. Lay out the two strips on newspaper with the best sides of the wood face down and apply a light, even coat of glue to one strip. Lightly dampen the other strip with a wet sponge, as this type of glue is activated by moisture. Working time using this type of glue is about eight to ten minutes.

12. Assemble the two strips and place the strips into the form with the cleats facing up. Place the first clamp in the middle of the form and start to tighten slowly so as not to crack the laminations. Apply a slow even pressure to compress the form.

13. Clamp each side with even pressure and continue to compress until the form is tight the full length of the laminations. Add more clamps if necessary to eliminate any voids between the laminations. Tighten all clamps. Set aside. Let dry for six hours.

14. When dry, loosen the clamps and remove the bent lamination. Carefully remove any glue squeezed out on the edges with a plane or a jointer. Watch the grain direction so you don't splinter the edges.

15. Draw the shape of the two tongs nested next to each other.

16. Carefully cut out the shapes on the band saw. With this bent shape, only two surfaces touch the table of the band saw. Hold the piece tight to the table and pass it through the blade. When sawing the ends, hold the shapes tight to the table.

17. Clean up the edges of the tongs on a smoothing plane mounted upside down in the bench vise. Watch the grain direction to prevent splintering. A couple passes over the plane will show whether you are going in the correct direction. If you notice tear out or splintering, turn the piece around and plane in the opposite direction. Seeing grain direction in thin pieces of wood is difficult.

18. Round over the edges with a sandpaper block and sand the surfaces with #220 grit paper. Make sure all glue spots are removed so they don't show up after the finish is applied.

For food-safe finishes for tongs, see page 151.

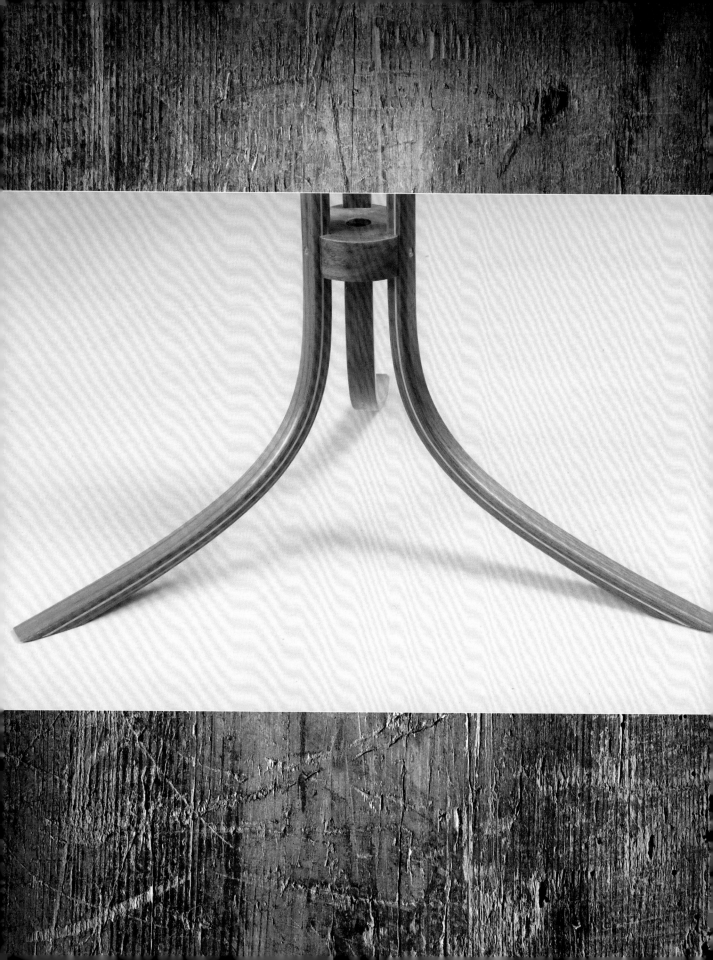

Making Larger
WOOD PROJECT Laminated Shapes

The legs used for this music stand are formed in a similar way to the salad tongs. The form is larger and more lamination strips are used. You can make your form any size or shape to meet your needs.

TOOLS

- table saw
- router
- straight router bit with a guide bearing
- band saw
- thickness planer
- jointer
- hand clamps
- polyurethane glue

EXPANDING THE FORM

When creating a bending form, make sure the bends or arcs are mild and not too severe. Make a full-size drawing of the shape. Then create some test lamination strips, bend them to match the drawing, and look for splits or cracking. If everything is acceptable, proceed by transferring the drawn arc to the form or pattern. Should there be bending problems, reduce the thickness of each strip or change the severity of the curve. Once the form is made, you cannot change it.

CHOOSE THE RIGHT GLUE

Choose the right glue: Epoxy and polyurethane glue are very stable and eliminate springback after the lamination is taken out of the clamps. White or yellow glues do not bond as well and can slip slightly when exposed to heat or humidity. Plastic resin glue is also used for laminations but is slightly toxic when mixing the powder with water. If you have breathing problems, it is best not to use resin glue.

CLAMPING THE CURVES

A good arsenal of heavy-duty clamps is needed when compressing the curved area on larger forms. These larger clamps are needed to eliminate any voids between the strips. An extra set of hands can be extremely helpful as well when doing large glue ups.

When making large bending forms, make sure the form is deep enough to accommodate wider material so you can cut two or three pieces from the same lamination. Cutting apart these curved forms is tricky and could be dangerous if not handled properly. For large or steep curves, stay away from the table saw. This is safer to do on a band saw or even a hand-held jig saw will get the job done.

(For more information on template-routing, see page 106.)

OPPOSITE "A nice set of legs" made with walnut and maple.

(continued on page 94)

MAKING THE FORM

Draw the proper shape onto a piece of ¾" MDF allowing room between male and female pieces to accommodate the thickness of the laminate strips.

Cut the shapes out using a band saw. Smooth out the shapes with files and sanding blocks. Use these pieces as templates and trace the shapes to other pieces of MDF. (The size and number of pieces will vary according to your project.)

Cut out the form shapes on a band saw allowing ¹⁄₁₆" extra beyond the traced line. Glue and clamp the template to the band-sawn pieces.

1. After they dry, clamp the form to your bench and place your router with the bearing riding on the template. The straight router bit will cut the over-sized pieces to the shape of the template.

2. Glue one side of the form to a base made of ¾" plywood or MDF. Leave the mating side loose so it can be clamped after the glued laminates are put in place. Glue cleats and screw to each side as a guide for proper alignment. Apply a sealer or shellac or wax to the form to prevent glue from sticking to the form. Mill the larger lamination strips the same way the strips for the salad tongs were (see page 90). To dress up the lamination, place a contrasting strip of maple between the layers of walnut strips. These strips should be 2¼" wide. This will allow for two 1" pieces to be cut on the table saw. If wider laminations are needed, make your form higher by adding more layers of MDF.

GLUING THE LAMINATION

3. Lay out strips and have clamps ready. You have about fifteen minutes before the glue sets. Apply polyurethane glue on alternating sides of the strips. Dampen the other side of the strips with water and then clamp in the form. It is wise to have help when doing this exercise. A practice run is advisable before final glue up.

4. Start clamping from the center of the curve. As the strips start to compress they will slide a little over each other. This way any slippage is transferred to each end equally. Think of it like squeezing a toothpaste tube from the middle! If your form has multiple bends, start from the middle and clamp out to each side. Leave extra length on the strips; they can be trimmed later. The laminate should stay clamped up for six hours.

5. Remove the bent laminate and carefully dress each side on the jointer to remove glue and smooth the edges.

6. Use push blocks to hold the shape against the fence to insure square edges.

7. Set the fence on the table saw to 1". Clamp a feather board to hold the 2¼" strip tight to the fence. Start ripping the curved end in a tipped up attitude keeping the strip flat on the table.

This cut can be a tricky maneuver on the table saw for the beginner. If you are not comfortable using the table saw for making this cut, try using the band saw:

- Scribe a center line on the piece.
- Raise the top blade guide up and place the piece flat on the table of the saw with the curve pointing up.
- Start your cut while keeping the back flat on the table for support.
- As you cut through the curve rotate the piece and continue to keep the surface on the table for support. Use a push stick to finish the cut. It would help to have an assistant to receive the piece as you finish the cut.

8. Use a push stick to follow through.

Veneered
WOOD PROJECT Flower Pendant

TOOLS

- hand clamps
- scroll saw
- yellow glue
- lathe
- CA glue
- ⅛" drill bit
- drill

Thin veneers that are glued together and compressed to shape are also considered lamination. To create this flower you will need some scraps of veneer. These can be ordered in small quantities from woodworking catalogs, or you can use them from other projects. You will also need a 4" × 8" piece of 1" rigid foam insulation.

Wood molding comes in many shapes. Most of these shapes can be used to form the petals for this pendant. Use a 6" piece of scrap molding and glue it to a 4" × 8" piece of plywood. Almost any molding will do as long as it has some curvature, such as crown or ogee pieces. Look for gentle curves rather than sharp angles. Scraps from the local home center are free. The wood can be oak, pine, or poplar. Do not use plastic coated Styrofoam, because it will crush. Wax the molding to prevent glue from sticking to it.

1A

1B

1. Apply yellow glue sparingly to four pieces of veneer, press them together, and place over the waxed molding. Alternate the grain direction of the veneers. This will give the petals strength and keep the veneers from cracking. Tape each side to hold the veneers in place.

(continued on page 98)

2A   2B   3   4

2. Before the glue sets, place a sheet of clear plastic wrap over the veneer to prevent the glue from sticking to the top form. Peel the plastic liner from one side of the foam 1"-thick insulation block and place the block over the clear plastic. Now the veneer is sandwiched between the molding, the plastic wrap, and the foam.

3. Place a 4" × 8" piece of plywood on top of the sandwich. Apply clamps to compress the sandwich. Tighten the clamps until the foam conforms to the shape of the molding. This compression will form the veneered layers to the shape of the molding.

4. After four hours, loosen the clamps. Remove the pieces of laminate and let them rest and dry for an hour.

5. Draw the shape of the petals on the curved veneer. Using a scroll saw and scissors, cut out the shape of the petals. This process can be repeated to make additional petals. Use different shapes of molding to vary the petal forms. Carefully sand with #220 grit paper and refine the petal edges with a sanding block.

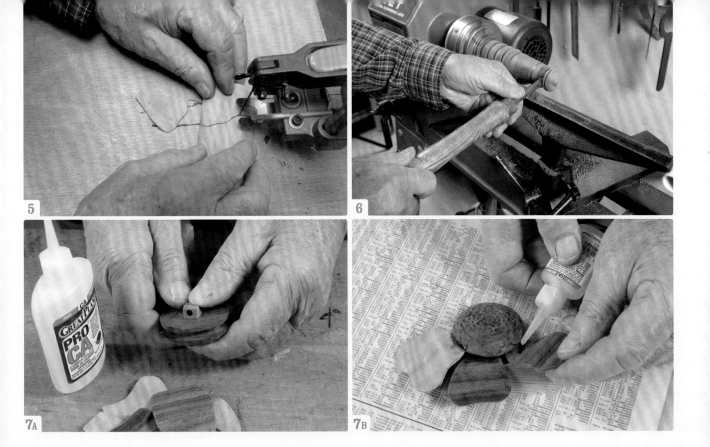

6. The hub can be turned on a lathe (see page 138) using a spindle gauge to form the domed top. A narrow groove is cut into the hub using a parting tool to receive the petals. To add interest to the hub, use a small veiner carving chisel (see page 120) to scoop out small dimples to give it texture. A small texturing tool tapped with light hammer strokes could also be used on the hub.

7. To attach the necklace, drill a 1/16" hole into a small block of wood and glue to the back of the hub using CA glue. Attach the petals to the hub with cyanoacrylate glue. Place them with alternating petals curling up and down for visual interest. See page 152 for information on the finish.

CHAPTER

6

Routers

Routers shape wood in a variety of ways. A handheld router can be passed over the work, or the wood can be shaped by being passed over a router mounted in a router table. The router cuts or shapes wood with router bits. It can be guided freehand or by using of a variety of jigs or fixtures to guide the spinning router bit.

Routers are high-speed motors that spin a cutting edged router bit. The motor is contained in a base that holds the motor to any predetermined depth of cut. The base is guided by hand or with an edge guide. Many of the cuts that are done on a table saw can also be achieved with the router.

They shape edges, cut many varieties of joinery, create matching parts, make inlays, bore holes, and cut circles and ovals. Routers can be attached to lathes to make flutes and spirals. Sign makers rout letters using templates of different styles and sizes.

Portable electric routers were invented during World War I. They were heavy and cumbersome, but they changed the way wood could be shaped. Today routers come in many forms, sizes, and power ratings, and they have become one of the most versatile tools in the woodshop.

An edge-forming Roman ogee profile bit is used on a tabletop with a fixed-base router. (A common tabletop edge, an ogee is a concave cut that reverses back to a straight edge.)

You can shape the edge of the work piece using a router bit with a decorative profile. You can create grooves or dados using straight bits. And in this chapter, you will learn how to guide these cutting bits by using a variety of attachments and guides.

Most manufacturers offer routers with electric motors that range from ½ horsepower (hp) to 3 hp. Some of these routers come with variable speeds ranging from 10,000 to 26,000 revolutions per minute (rpm). Many routers have interchangeable collets for using ¼" and ½" shank router bits. Smaller handheld trim routers accommodate only ¼" shank router bits. Today's routers are equipped with soft start motors that help reduce the whipping torque when turning on the router.

Basic Router Styles

The **fixed-base router** allows the motor to travel up or down within the base to set the depth of the cut. An incremental adjusting guide sets the cutting depth. A clamping mechanism locks the motor body to the base. The base has two opposing handles or a handle that the operator grasps to guide the router. An edge guide attachment keeps the router bit square to the edge of the work piece. The edge guide is attached to the router base with rods that allow for in and out adjusting. The fixed-base router is also used to mount underneath a router table.

Some fixed-base routers have a removable base that can be interchanged with a plunge router base. Most manufacturers now offer these combination options, which save you from having to buy two routers. These versatile routers have interchangeable collets to enable the use of ¼" or ½" shank router bits.

The **dedicated plunge router** is used for making mortise and tenon joints, stopped dado grooves, and hinge mortises. The motor rides on posts that connect to the base using spring tension. The depth of cut is governed by a bar that rests on an adjustable turret stop. The depth of cut on a plunge router can be changed in mid operation without the need to turn off the machine. There is a plunge lock lever that can be manually activated to stop the downward action to the appropriate depth. The fixed-base router is preset to cut a specific depth. To change the depth of cut, the fixed-base router has to be turned off and unplugged to reset the depth of cut.

Smaller **palm routers** are ideal for laminate trimming, sign making, grooving, and edge forming. They are lightweight and easy to handle. Most have only ¼" collets. Some manufacturers offer offset and tilt bases as well as edge guides as accessories.

Router Bits

Router bits come in hundreds of sizes and profiles. Most bits consist of a steel body with cutting edges and a shank that fits into the collet in the router. The shanks come in ¼"- or ½"-diameter sizes. Some inexpensive router bits are made of high-speed steel, but most router bits are made of carbide steel. They are more expensive, but are sharper and longer lasting and invaluable for cutting hardwoods and manmade materials.

| TIP |
Router Speed

Your router has a range of speeds to choose from. A rule of thumb is that the larger the diameter of the bit, the slower the speed and the smaller the diameter bit, the higher the speed. A large router bit carries more surface area and weighs more. And so if it rotates at high speed and contacts the wood, there could be a severe kickback and the piece could be torn from your hands. A large router bit rotating at high speed could also vibrate and loosen itself from the collet and be expelled from the router.

Smaller diameter router bits can run at higher speeds because there is less centrifugal force. The higher speed will offer a smoother cut. The wood must be fed evenly past the spinning bit without slowing down, which could create a burn mark.

Some fixed-base routers have a removable base that can be interchanged with a plunge router base. Most manufacturers now offer these combination options, which save you from having to buy two routers. These versatile routers have interchangeable collets to enable the use of ¼" or ½" shank router bits.

Router bits can be purchased separately to cut specific shapes. There are starter kits available that offer 10 or more of the most-often-used shapes. This is an economical way to start your bit collection. These bits come in either ¼"- or ½"-diameter shanks. As a rule ½" shank bits are a little more expensive than ¼" bits. For higher horsepower routers, ½" shanks are recommended. The cost difference between ¼" and ½" shanks is negligible. The larger molding type bits are all ½" shanks.

Always clean and inspect your bits after you use them. Check the carbide edges to make sure there are no chips or cracks. Damaged bits can be dangerous and should be discarded. When carbide tipped bits become dull they can be resharpened with diamond files or sent to a professional sharpening service. Check the collets every time you change bits. Sawdust and pitch can build up in the tapers and prevent proper seating. A small wire brush and a blast from the air hose can make the collets lock tight around the shank of the router bit.

Larger router table bits are heavier than bits used in handheld routers. They all have ½" shanks because of their weight and size. These bits are made for cutting crown moldings, cope and stick joints, raised panels, chair rails, and large ogee moldings.

TIP | Tighten to Prevent Slippage

Check for router bit slippage: After you tighten the router bit in the collet, draw a vertical line on the shaft of the bit and the collet with a fine-tipped marker. Make some test cuts and stop the router to check the scribed line. If the marks do not line up, there has been some slippage. Take out the bit and clean the collet with a brass wire brush. Reinstall the bit and tighten the collet.

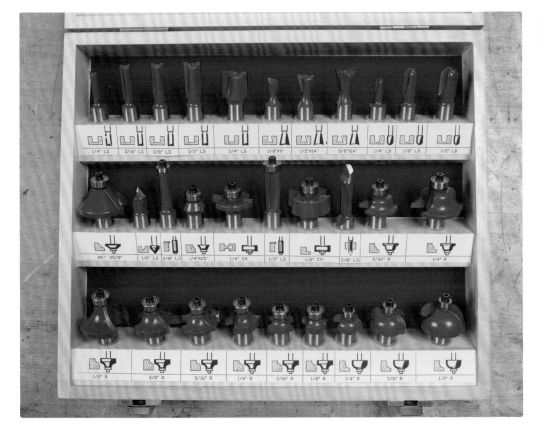

A thirty-piece router bit starter kit is an economical way to start your router collection.

LEFT + BELOW It is important to store your router bits properly. They should be separated by shank diameter on a surface with holes drilled to keep the bits upright and not hitting each other.

A drawer ensures you have easy access to the full selection. Accessories paired with the router bits include different diameter bearings for adjusting the depth of cuts, and router bushing guides.

TIP | Feeling Groovy

When routing using a grooving bit, don't try to cut too deep in one pass. Make depth cuts of no more than 1/8" at a time. This will eliminate burning, ragged edges, and save your router bits. When routing across the grain on plywood it is advisable to carefully score the edges of the width of cut with a sharp blade. This will eliminate the ragged fibers on the edges of the groove.

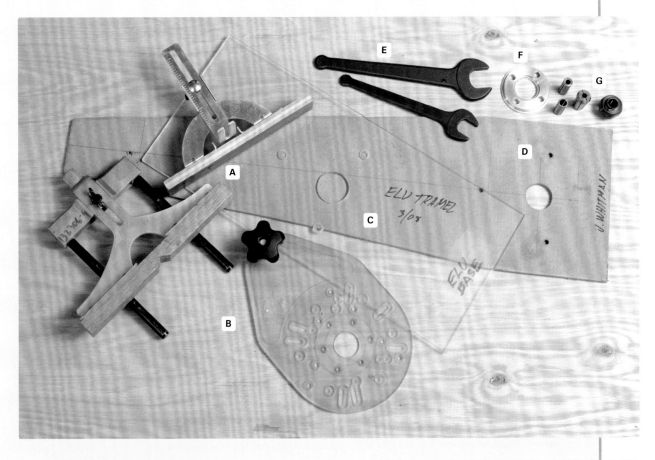

▲ **There are many accessories and adaptors that can be used with your routers to make them more versatile. Many of these accessories can be made in your shop using plywood, MDF, and Plexiglas.**

A. Edge guides with wooden edges added

B. Offset base plate for stability while routing

C. Oversize Plexiglas base plate made for stability over a large area being routed

D. Circle jig made of MDF

E. Extra set of collet wrenches

F. Base plate adaptors for different sizes of template guides

G. Extra set of collets

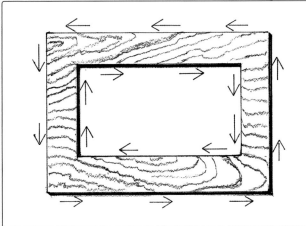

Routing Direction

When routing the outside edge of a board, always cut in a counterclockwise direction. When routing the inside of a shape, move in a clockwise direction. When cutting on a router table, move the workpiece against the router bit.

TECHNIQUE:
Using Routing Patterns and Templates

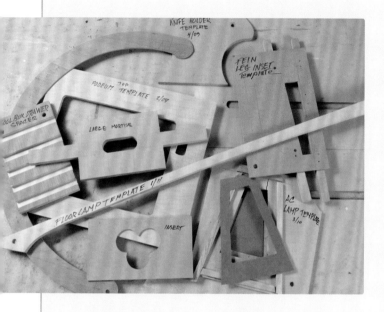

To route on or in materials, a pattern or template is needed to guide the router bit to cut the appropriate shape. Template guides or bearings will follow the shape or contour of the templates.

Templates can be made from a variety of materials, and you can custom-make them for your project or buy them premade. The most commonly used material is MDF because it is easy to machine and shape. Other materials used are plywood, plastics, and hard board such as Masonite.

The templates or patterns can be affixed to the material to be cut in many ways.

- Attach the template to the work piece using two-sided tape.
- Clamp the template and work piece into a jig to run on the router table.
- Attach guides to the template to register and locate it onto the work piece.
- A pin nailer (page 59) can be used to secure the template to the work. Use only a few pins to secure the template as this will enable easy removal.

ABOVE Always keep your templates and patterns for repeat work. Label and date the templates with the name of your project.

BELOW, LEFT There are many ways to fabricate templates. One way is to cut the shape from a solid piece of material. There are easier ways to create the appropriate shapes. Precut the shapes and then assemble them as a unit.

BELOW, RIGHT Glue and clamp the precut shapes to make the finished template. Note the extensions left to enable clamping.

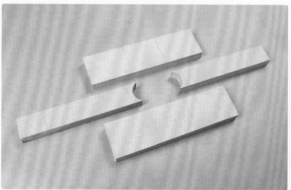

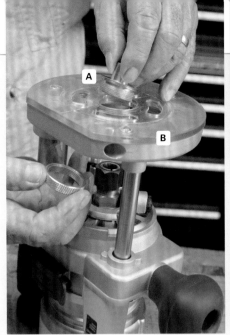

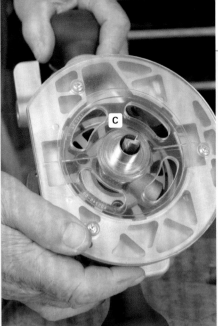

RIGHT The template guide bushing (A) is attached to the base plate of the router (B). There is a collar that screws onto the bushing that is nested in the router base.

FAR RIGHT The straight bit (C) is now inserted into the collet and tightened. The straight bit can protrude through the guide bushing to the proper depth of cut. You cannot use a bearing guided bit with this bushing set up.

TEMPLATE GUIDES

Template guides are attached to the router base plate. The straight router bit rotates inside the guide bushing. The diameter of the bit should be close to the inside dimension of the bushing without touching the cutting edges. The bushing can now ride against the template. Guide bushings should only be used with straight router bits.

PATTERN ROUTING WITH BEARING PILOT BITS

Edge forming bits use pilot bearings to guide them along edges or to follow template shapes. Most larger router table bits have bearings to guide wood against. Different size bearings can be added to router bits to change the width of cut.

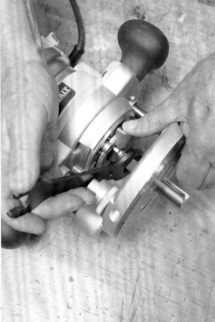

FAR LEFT The author inserts a straight bit with a pilot bearing into the collet of the plunge router; note the turret depth stop on the left.

LEFT A thumb-pressed shaft-locking mechanism holds the drive shaft tight while the collet is locked in place. Now the base can be adjusted to the proper height or depth.

Making Decorative Inlays

Inlaying shapes of contrasting wood onto furniture, boxes, and accessories is a laborious, complex task. The process is called intarsia. A simpler way to inlay larger and less intricate shapes is to use an inlay bushing set attached to the base plate of the router. A ⅛" spiral bit rotates inside the bushing to cut the recess, and the bushing rides against the template. By modifying the bushing, you can use the router to cut a matching inlay piece in another piece of wood using the same template.

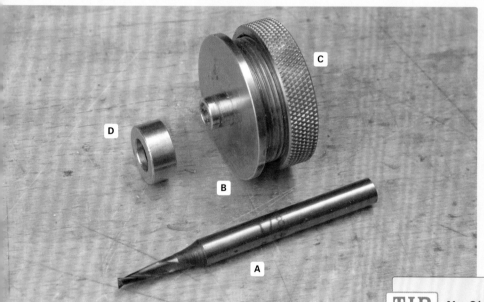

The pattern inlay kit consists of four parts: the ⅛" diameter spiral bit (A), the brass template guide (B), the locking ring (C), and the detachable large guide (D).

TOOLS

- fixed base router
- ⅛" diameter carbide spiral bit
- a brass inlay bushing set
- ½" diameter straight bit
- ¼" thick template of your choice

TIP | No Sharp Corners

When making your own templates, make sure all edges are true and smooth. Any lump or bump will be telegraphed to your workpiece. A template made with sharp corners will not allow the template guide to follow a sharp corner because the guide is round. Hand work will be needed to chisel or cut the sharp corners.

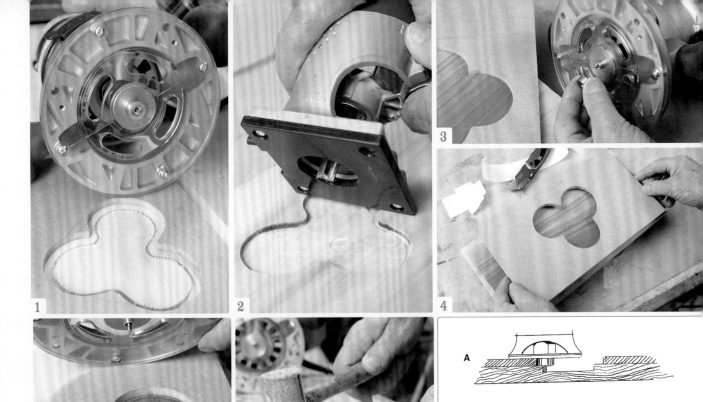

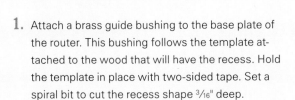

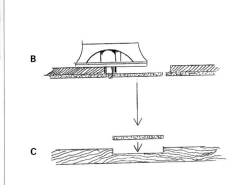

1. Attach a brass guide bushing to the base plate of the router. This bushing follows the template attached to the wood that will have the recess. Hold the template in place with two-sided tape. Set a spiral bit to cut the recess shape $3/16$" deep.

2. With a $1/2$" straight bit on a small palm router, excavate the wood inside of the outlined shape. Set the depth of cut to $3/16$". A palm router (or any small-size router) allows you to see where the router bit is cutting. Be careful not to cut the edges of the recess.

3. Remove the larger bushing from the guide. The smaller bushing will follow the same template used to cut the recess in order to create the inlay workpiece.

4. Place the template on the inlay piece of wood using two-sided tape. The $1/4$" thick inlay wood should be taped to a backer board.

The anatomy of the inlay process.

A. Route the recess with the large bushing following the template.

B. Remove large bushing. Using the same template, route the stock for the insert.

C. Now the insert can be placed in the previously routed recess.

5. With the smaller diameter guide bushing, follow the template to cut the walnut inlay piece.

6. Place the inlay into the recess. The fit should be nice and snug. Apply glue and tap the piece with a small mallet, if necessary.

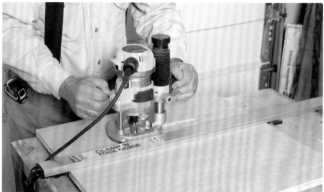

Using a Router Table

There are many sizes and shapes of router tables on the market. A router table equipped with a powerful router can create a vast array of shapes for furniture and architectural uses. There are special routers on the market that are designed for use only in the router table. They contain controls to raise and lower the router from above without reaching under the table to adjust the height or change bits.

The availability of hundreds of router bit shapes can make crown molding, chair rails, and all forms of molding. These bits can be used in combination with other bits to deliver some pretty impressive shapes.

BUY A ROUTER TABLE

There are many commercially made router tables available. Some are small tabletop models that offer dust collection ports, adjustable fences, safety shields, and a miter gauge track. The larger cabinet-type models offer larger tabletops, higher adjustable fences, and aluminum insert plates for router mounting. These tables range widely in price. A shop-made router table can be designed and built to meet the woodworker's needs.

FAR LEFT Using a plunge router with an edge guide holds the router in place while making repetitive cuts; you can adjust the depth of cut on each pass.

TOP, RIGHT A shop-built circle cutting jig can be adjusted to cut any size circle desired. The pivot point can be placed at any point on the center line to change the diameter of the cut.

ABOVE RIGHT An edge guide clamp is used to guide the router.

Router Safety

There are safety precautions needed when working on a router table. You are passing wood through a high-speed, rotating cutter. Always use push blocks and feather boards to secure the piece you are routing. Never use gloves as they can be easily caught by the cutter and can draw your hand or finger into harm's way. Roll up your sleeves or button your cuffs. Remove any bracelets or rings.

Holding jigs can be made for securing small pieces while routing on the table. There are commercially made holders available for securing small objects. Never introduce the front of your piece into the spinning cutter unless it is supported by the bearing and the fence.

Always wear safety glasses and hearing protection when using your router.

Build Your Own Router Table

If you prefer to make a table, there are plans available from most woodworking magazines to make any size or style table to suit your needs.

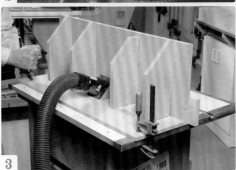

Aftermarket parts are available to build a strong, safe table. Tables feature dust collection ports and T-track material to hold an endless variety of jigs and fixtures. Drop-in base plates are designed to receive a variety of routers. They are made of aluminum or plastic.

The tabletop can be made of MDF/Melamine and the edge banded with solid wood. You can route a slot on the top to hold feather boards or a miter gauge. There are many varieties of fences on the market or you can build your own. Keeping safety in mind, install an on/off switch on the outside of the table.

1. Attach a solid base plate to the router and drop it into the tabletop in the routed recess.

2. Different diameter insert plates are used to accommodate large or small router bits.

3. A rugged homemade fence will stay square to the tabletop. This one is made with MDF, glued, and screwed. Connect a dust collection port to a shop vacuum. The fence is held in place with shop clamps after adjustments have been set. The height of the fence allows for tall panels to be routed.

4. Use a straight edge to set the fence parallel to the bearing on the router bit. Tighten the rear clamps. Notice the miter gauge slot routed into the table top. The slot also works well to hold a feather board attachment.

Routing Cope and Stick Joints for Door Frames

The router table is ideal for making rail and stile joinery for door frames. This joint is also referred to as cope and stick. The rail and stile router bits come in matched sets. Each set has its own style of cut: ogee, round over, beading, traditional, French provincial, and Shaker. These sets can also include bits to rout matching raised panels.

These photos show the appropriate bit that is used to cut each contour. The fence has been set back to expose the entire router bit.

1. Use a miter gauge with a wood backer to cut the end of the rail. This prevents tear out at the end of the cut. The edge of the rail rides on the bearing in between the top and bottom cutters.

2. Change the bit to make the stile cut. The board should run against the fence and the bearing. The groove that runs the length of the rail and stile will house the door panel.

3. The rail and stile contours provide a good glue surface area for strong joints.

TIP | Make Extra Rails

Always make extra rails and stiles for making test cuts. A nice fit makes a nice door.

Dovetails Made
WOOD PROJECT **with the Router**

Using this jig in combination with a fixed-base router, you can create many variations of dovetail joints. You can make half-blind dovetails, through dovetails, sliding dovetails, and box joints. This segment will deal with making half-blind dovetails to create drawers or boxes. This set up will cut the pin board (front) and tail board (side) at the same time. (This set up was used on page 83 to make the drawer for the Shaker end table.)

TOOLS

- half-blind dovetail template, $^{17}/_{32}$"
- 7 degree dovetail bit, $^{3}/_{4}$" outside dimension
- template guide and lock nut
- a fixed base router with a ½" collet
- The dovetail bit and template guide are supplied by the manufacturer.

If you purchase this jig for your shop, excellent set up directions are included. There are several other manufacturers that offer similar systems for making dovetails. Check your woodworking magazines and catalogs for more details and price comparisons.

Mill the side, front, and back boards to the same thickness and height. Cut the two side boards to the exact length needed, and cut the front and back boards the same length as needed. Make sure all ends are square and the boards are milled perfectly flat. Mark all boards on one side to identify the outside surfaces.

1. The bushing guide rides along the finger-shaped template while the dovetail bit extends below to cut to the proper depth.

2. The dovetail jig has the front and side pieces already routed or cut. Note the bushing guide with the dovetail bit extending beyond it to the proper cutting depth.

Carving
Wood

Carving wood is a great way to start out in your woodworking endeavors.
You don't need a large area to work in, there is no need for heavy machinery, and it is a quiet way to work. And you can develop a specialty niche as your skills increase. Carving decoys, birds, and fish will lead you into painting them and woodburning to create feathering. Another specialty to develop is carving signs and lettering. Or you could explore chip carving, which is a highly specialized technique using special knives rather than chisels.

Carving has historically been an important part of the furniture-making industry, and during the seventeenth and eighteenth centuries, furniture makers were also wood carvers. Historical pieces are often embellished with seashells, flowing acanthus leaves, C scrolls, lion heads, grape clusters, and figures. Chair and table legs were carved with the popular ball and claw motifs. Even the ship-building industry enlisted wood carvers to decorate their beautiful windjammer sailing ships.

The author carving
a self portrait.

Styles of Carving

These images are not carved deeply into the surface. They show great detail without requiring the removal of a lot of wood.

Low relief. Carving on the surface of wood is classified as shallow or low relief. An example of this is carving letters for a sign. Carving an image with great detail but with shallow wood removal is also classified as low relief. Low relief carving is usually done on two to three levels of wood removal. A field or background sets off the higher levels of the image.

High relief. Deeper carvings with more dimension and removal of deeper layers of wood are called high relief carving. One of the challenges of high relief carving is determining what part of the carving is closer to you and what parts are farther away. This decision will give your carving more dimension. If you combine this type of carving with perspective, you can achieve a more realistic image even though it is not carved in the round.

Carving in the round. The most challenging carving technique is carving in the round, or sculpture. To create an accurate carving in the round, your visual reference material must give you 360 degrees of information. A series of photos of the object will aid in this.

The ball and claw images are called carving in the round because they are more sculptural or three dimensional. The carvers who crafted animals for classic carousels carved in the round, too.

Making a half- or quarter-size clay model will also help you visualize your carving in the round subject.

You will also be faced with carving in end grain as well as many grain changes as you work around the wood. You cannot carve from one position or in one direction. You must be able to approach the carving from different directions or be able to manipulate the carving to make the wood easy to access. It may take practice, but using many different tools and working many different designs or carving lines will improve your techniques.

To prepare wood for carving a silhouette, you will need a band saw to cut out the profile or shape to eliminate as much of the unwanted wood as possible. More unwanted wood could be removed from the carving block using a grinder or rasps (see page 124).

Swiss-made chisels seem to hold a sharper edge longer. Some chisels are sharp out of the box; others need some honing to bring them up to speed. Even if you get lucky and find a good set of chisels at a garage sale or flea market, it might need sharpening before you use it.

Your initial tool purchase should include a sharpening system. An economical way to start is a set of medium and fine oil stones, a small can of oil, and a piece of leather to strop your chisels. You could also invest in diamond plates or water stones. Using any of these systems will take some experimenting to be able to maintain razor-sharp knives and chisels. Learning proper sharpening techniques will also help you to sharpen plane blades and bench chisels.

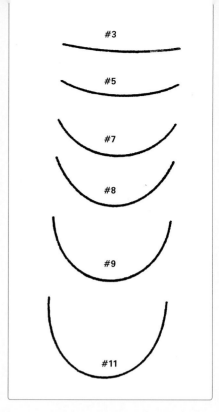

BELOW A set of carving knives aid in the carving process.

RIGHT Sweep numbers indicate the shape of the gouge. The lower the number, the shallower the gouge.

Sharpening:
THE SECRET TO CARVING SUCCESS

After you acquire carving chisels, they will likely have to be honed. Even newly purchased chisels are not truly sharp out of the box. And if an edge is destroyed or chipped, you will need to grind it. Grinding, working through coarser grits or using a grinding wheel, shapes the edge. Honing, or further refining the shaped edge by working through the finer grits, sharpens it. Honing is always the final step.

To sharpen your tools, first grind them as necessary. Then, hone them using a fine grit surface (1000+ grits). This should produce a burr, or a thin sliver of metal left on the edge of the chisel. After a burr is achieved by honing, remove it using a leather strop or buffing wheel. (This technique was once used by barbers when they stropped their razors on the leather band.) Sharpening will take practice, but once it is mastered, carving will become much easier.

There are three choices for sharpening knives, chisels, and gouges:

A. oil stones
B. diamond plates and files
C. water stones
D. leather pad for stropping (which is used in all three methods)

TIP | **Use a Jeweler's Loop**

Use a jeweler's loop (a small hand-held magnifying glass) to check the edge of your chisels. This will magnify any flat spots or irregularities, and you will be able to correct them.

1

2

3

There are many methods of using grinding and honing to sharpen knives and chisels. Three basic systems use oil stones, water stones, and diamond plates. Any of these provide coarse, medium, and fine grit surfaces.

1. Using a combination of diamond plates and water stones will hasten the sharpening process. If some reshaping (in case of chipping) is needed, use diamond plates lubricated with water. Work through all the grits on the plates to the finest grit, which is indicated by the green dot. When you can feel a burr on the edge of the chisel, you are almost there.

2. Switch to the finer water stones. These stones range from 600 grit to 4000 grit. Using the finer stone will put a mirror finish on the edge of the chisel. This should produce a fine burr or lip that can be felt with your finger.

3. To eliminate the wire edge, move to the leather stropping pad and stroke both sides of the edge back and forth until the burr is eliminated.

Different shaped carving tools take different approaches when being sharpened. When sharpening or honing gouges, the angled surface on the leading edge is the area to be sharpened. A sweeping, rolling, back and forth motion on the edge of this angled surface should be presented to the stone. When a fine burr appears on the edge, it is time to hone on the leather strop.

V parting tools and flat chisels are sharpened differently than gouges; these tools are held flat against the sharpening surface to achieve a sharp edge. The beveled edge and the flat backs are both honed to form a wire edge that is then stropped. There are jigs that clamp the chisels to hold them at the proper bevel angle while working them over the various sharpening stones.

These are some of the many techniques by many experts that are used to achieve the sharp edge. After some experimenting, you will find the technique that is best for you.

To put an edge on a sweep gouge, hold the tool at about 30 degrees and sweep it back and forth on the edge until the burr appears. Hone on the leather strop.

More Carving Tool Options

There are other tools that can aid in the carving process. Here are some options to explore as you develop your personal carving process and preferences.

A. Spoke shaves: The spoke shave acts like a miniature plane. The blade can be adjusted to give fine or coarse cuts. The spoke shave can be used to smooth out large areas without leaving tool marks and can eliminate a lot of wood quickly.

B. Card scrapers: Card scrapers are an ideal tool to use to eliminate tool marks and rough areas that appear in carvings made with gouges and chisels. There is a limit to the area the scraper can reach due to its shape. Scrapers also come in convex and concave shapes.

C. Flexible shaft grinders: If you want to eliminate wood fast, this is the system to use. These flexible shaft grinders, which can accept many different styles and shapes of cutting bits, are used to eliminate wood when undercutting areas of your carving. The cutter can get into areas where chisels cannot. Most grinders can be outfitted with a variable speed control foot pedal. Grinding creates a lot of dust, so wear safety glasses and a dust mask.

D. Rasps: The rasp or file is used to shape wood quickly. Rasps come in flat, curved, or round profiles. They also come with fine, medium, or coarse surfaces. Rasps are used for shaping large surfaces found in sculptural carving.

E. Rifflers: The rifflers are miniature files that come in many shapes that fit into areas that need to be refined or smoothed out. The riffler helps to clean out rough areas that chisels cannot fit into. They are made for fine detail work.

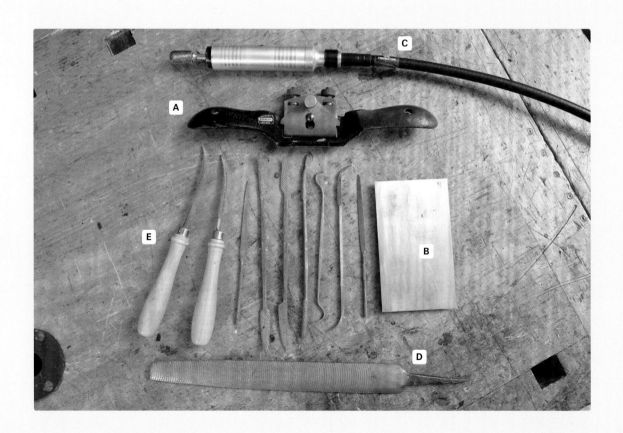

Setting Up Your Project

Before you begin carving, make sure your space and tools are set up in the way that's most comfortable. There are a few essentials. The first is a stable bench or table to work on with a clamping system to secure the piece you are working on and room to keep your tools neatly arranged while carving. The tool holder panel in the photo at right, for example, keeps the chisels off the bench while carving and is removable when not in use. Small shelves support the tools, while magnetic strips secure them. Chisels tips are easily damaged if they are all left on the bench top clanging and bumping into each other. Good lighting is also a must to distinguish the details.

There are many ways to secure your wood while carving. Two can be seen in the photo below. On the right is a handmade T-stand that can be raised, lowered, or tilted in the vise. The top has coarse, adhesive-backed sandpaper applied to it, which stops slippage while the work piece is clamped to it. There are holes in the top that allows a skew (a large tapered screw) to be used to secure a larger piece of wood for carving. The bench clamp on the left can be raised or lowered to secure thick or thin wood to the workbench. The work piece can be easily rotated and reclamped. The bench clamp is also used to secure wood when chopping dovetails.

And it is important to be comfortable while carving. Bending over for several hours can wreak havoc on the back. Some carvers even use a tilting table system that allows them to sit upright while carving.

A tool holder panel keeps chisels organized and out of harm's way. Also notice the T-stand at a comfortable height for making stop cuts.

Two ways to secure your work while carving: a T-stand (right) and a bench clamp (left).

Beginning Your Project

There is no lack of subject matter when you are starting to carve. You don't have to be an artist; you just need strong visual references that you can duplicate on wood. There are many commercial patterns and drawings available. Books containing royalty-free patterns have thousands of designs and patterns to work from. And, if you want to create your own original pattern, use your digital camera to capture an object or pattern. You can then print the photo, transfer the image to wood (as outlined below), and then carve it.

Reference books and drawings made from your research can inspire you in choosing your subject matter.

1. Having drawing skills is a plus (although not necessary), because you won't be limited to the specific subject matter found in pattern books. Draw your pattern at a comfortable size (A). Use a photocopier to enlarge or reduce the pattern to carving size.

2. Tape the image to the wood (B).

3. Slip a piece of carbon paper between the copy and the wood. Some carvers use spray adhesive on the back of the copy and then apply it to the wood. It is a good idea to have an extra set of copies to refer to should the original become damaged from regular retracing.

4. Trace the image onto the wood.

5. As you start to carve, keep a practice board to see how the wood reacts to different chisel shapes (C). Test cutting across the grain as well as with the grain. This process is like keeping a three-dimensional sketchbook. This is a good place to practice the depth of cuts to establish high and low areas of an image.

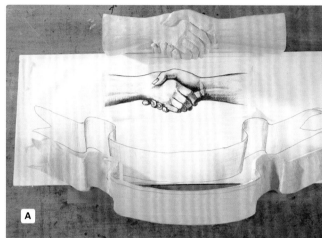

A

B

C

> **TIP** | **Pushpins as Register Marks**
>
> While the image is taped to the board, use a pushpin and place two or three holes through the image and into the wood. The holes should be outside of the image area. These holes will act as register marks to replace the drawing to retrace lost pencil lines while carving.

Leaf
WOOD PROJECT **Scroll**

Leaf scrolls date back to the ancient Greek and Roman eras. Acanthus leaves and leaf scrolls were carved in wood and stone. This type of design still thrives today in architecture and furniture design worldwide. The flowing, graceful leaves can be blended with other forms to accent any given shape. They can flow and bend to accent picture frames or chair legs. Think of this image as a bendable, pliable form that can be designed to fit anywhere. Now you can try your drawing skills to copy the image used for this lesson on paper and transfer it on the wood using carbon paper.

TOOLS AND MATERIALS

- ¾" mahogany or basswood
- scroll saw or band saw
- carbon paper
- clamp
- mallet
- #3, #5, #7 gouges
- knife
- V gouge

1. Transfer the scroll pattern to a piece of mahogany, and cut the outside arc on the band saw. Match the gouge sweeps to the curves on the pattern. Make the stop cuts, being careful not to crush the narrow stems. Use a lighter-weight mallet to tap the delicate cuts.

2. Relieve the background wood with gouges that have a flatter sweep. This will help to keep the background flat and even. Watch the grain direction as you cut around the curves. If you detect any tear out, cut from another direction. You can now start to scallop the leaves to give them some shape using a small #7 gouge.

(continued on page 128)

3. Use the V gouge to cut the thin veining. Remember to change direction as you cut around the curves. Cut with the grain, not into it. This is a delicate exercise but a necessary one to accomplish. Here again is a good opportunity to clean up with riffler files.

4. After you finish the detailing of the scroll and the leaves, finish the background with a gradual taper into the field that surrounds the image. Sand the contoured edge and the background. Now apply yellow milk paint and let it dry. Then apply any dark, contrasting color and let that dry. Come back with #220-grit sandpaper and sand lightly. This will reveal the under color in the high areas to give the carving an aged look.

WOOD PROJECT Head

The bald eagle is an iconic subject for many wood carvers. It has been carved in many poses, combined with flags, arrows, anchors, ribbons, and more, and with open and closed wings.

Ship carvers adorned many ships with eagles as a figurehead, and it was also seen on the tailboard (or the nameplate on the stern) and every place in between.

This project will be devoted to only the eagle's head. Carve a pair of these heads and you can make bookends. As you progress in your skills, the whole eagle (and a whole menagerie of animal figures) awaits you.

TOOLS AND MATERIALS

- ¾" basswood
- carbon paper
- band saw
- clamps
- mallet
- #3, #5, #7 chisels
- knife
- V gouge

A simple outline drawing can be enough reference for some people to work from. Other carvers need a more detailed sketch to show highlight and shadow. This eagle head will be used to refer to while carving.

(continued on page 130)

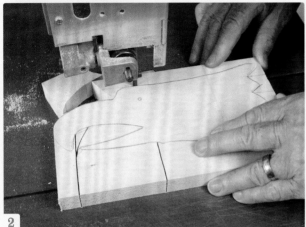

1. Make a drawing of an eagle head as per the drawing shown on page 129. The eagle can be traced onto the wood using the carbon paper slipped under the drawing. You can also make a template to outline the image, which will save you a lot of time if you plan on making several carvings. I made a plastic template to use in my carving classes.

2. Cut out the outline drawn on the basswood with a band saw. If you don't have a band saw, a hand scroll saw could be used to cut out the head. Stay on or a hair to the outside of the pencil line. You can always carve back to the line, but it's hard to add wood once you have cut it away.

3. To add details, such as the feathers, eye, and beak profile, choose a gouge that closely matches the shape of the feather ends. Make stop cuts using the mallet to send the gouge into the wood about 1/8". (Stop cuts allow you to carve up to the cut without tearing away wood that you want to preserve.) Use other shaped gouges to delineate between the beak and head. Use a knife to outline other shapes the gouges don't match. (Note: the clamp has been eliminated from the photo for clarity.)

4. Start to scoop away the wood by directing the gouge into the stop cuts. Be careful not to undercut the stop cuts, which happens when the stop cut is not cut squarely; this allows the edge of the cut to overhang the relieved area, making it weak and brittle. Using the different shaped sweeps, start to cut away and form a contour to the head. Watch grain direction—no tear outs, please! Keep turning the carving to get a better carving angle or when you encounter a grain problem. (Note: the clamp has been eliminated from the photo for clarity.)

5. To make the veins in the feathers, use a V gouge, which is great for detail work. It will work well for cleaning up edges and getting into corners. The V tool will help in the detail work around the eyes as well. Rifflers will also come in handy by cleaning up corners and eliminating some of the ragged edges. (Note: the clamp has been eliminated from the photo for clarity.)

6. Another way to hold the eagle for carving would be to use two-sided carpet tape to secure it to a piece of plywood. The plywood could then be clamped to the work area. It could then be removed from the plywood when you are finished carving.

There are many ways to finish the eagle carving. After all the detail has been carved, sand the surface around the beak, lower jaw, and crown to smooth out any tool marks. Don't sand the feathers, as you will eliminate the detail you just added with the V tool. Apply your choice of finish.

Simple
WOOD PROJECT Flower

This flower carving is another example of low relief carving and will show you how to get more dimension into a shallow carving. Each petal is on a different plane from the others and will curve down to the center hub. You can copy any kind of flower for this project.

TOOLS AND MATERIALS

- ¾" basswood or mahogany
- carbon paper
- clamps
- #3, #5, #7 gouges
- knife
- V gouge
- mallet

1. Trace or draw the flower onto the selected wood. Using the appropriate chisels to match the drawing, start making stop cuts about an ⅛" deep. A knife can be used to cut the long arcs of the stems. (Note: the clamp has been eliminated for clarity.)

2. Carve away the background using a shallow gouge such as a #3 or #5. Carefully cut up to the stop cuts but not into the stems or petals. As you carve around the flower you compensate your cutting directions to match grain direction. Now is the time to prepare an even, flat background.

3. Start carving the petals so they scoop down into the center hub. Every other petal should be relieved lower than the adjacent petal. This will start to give dimension to the flower. Try to keep in mind what part of the flower is closest to you and what part is farther away. The center hub can be rounded. Remember how the grain direction changes as you carve around the curve of the hub. You can start to put a little curvature on the tip of each petal: some curve up and some curve down. This can be done with a #7 gouge.

4. Smooth out all the petals, stems, and leaves with the appropriate chisels. Use the V tool to crisp all the edges. Here is another opportunity to use the different shaped rifflers to smooth and clean up where needed. Use the V gouge to put in the veining on the petals. This simple flower will show you how to achieve dimension in a ⅜" deep low relief carving.

5. The detailing of the flower is your choice. The petals could be carefully undercut to give them a lighter feel, but care should be taken not to get too thin because the edges of the petals will become too fragile. Detailing of the center button could be achieved with some texture. A blunt nail tapped with light hammer blows will do this. Use a #3 scoop chisel to smooth the background field to contrast with the texture of the flower. Only sand the background to contrast with the flower. A clear finish could be used to show off the mahogany.

Turning
Wood

If your woodworking space is limited, turning is an ideal discipline to pursue. Like carving, it doesn't take up a lot of space. If you plan on turning small objects such as bottle stoppers or pens, your work can even be portable. If you use a mobile base on your lathe, you can work on your deck or porch on a beautiful day.

Simple projects to start with are objects such as tops, candlesticks, bottle stoppers, and bowls. Intricate turning techniques are being used to create forms that are puzzling to a beginning turner, inspiring and challenging them at the same time. Some of the more intricate turning procedures are off-center turning, hollow vessels, segmented bowls, and spherical or egg shapes. The endless array of tricks and techniques available to wood turners is what drives beginners to become proficient in such a popular discipline.

Wood was being turned as far back as 3000 BCE. The earliest lathes were created using a bow with the bowstring wrapped taut around the object to be turned. The wooden rod was rotated between a support at each end. This made turning difficult because the cutting tool was held in one hand while the bow was worked back and forth with the other. This method is still used today in some parts of India. The turner holds the tool with his foot and one hand while he works the bow back and forth with his other hand.

Around 1500 CE, Leonardo da Vinci invented a lathe made of wood and metal that relied on a crankshaft for steady, consistent movement. This allowed the wood to be rotated toward the tool, but only in one direction. Later, lathes were made of wood and a foot treadle was used to power the turning spindle. The addition of a tool rest made the task a lot simpler.

During the industrial revolution, lathes were made of cast iron and were driven by transmission belts. Then came the electric motor, and here we are today.

In this chapter, we will discuss what you need to know to get started in simple spindle and bowl wood turning. These are the basic steps that will lead you more intricate work in the future. As with so many other woodworking techniques, you can learn just so much from a book. It's the hands-on time at the lathe where you will learn to make your tools do what you want.

Materials for Turning

Wood is the most popular material used for turning, followed by plastics, other synthetic materials, soft stone, bone, and metal. Wood used for turning can be anything from freshly cut green wood in a variety of backyard species to old wood that is nearly rotten. As different species of wood dry, shrink, and crack, they create new variables (or design opportunities) for turners. As you learned in chapter 2, there are heartwoods, sapwoods, burls, spalted woods, softwoods, and hardwoods, all with different colors and grain patterns. These variables should be taken into account when designing your turning project.

 What's Hot in Turning?

One of the most popular turning disciplines today is turning pen and pencil sets. This has grown into an industry all unto itself. There are special mini and midi lathes available, highly patterned turning stock, and pen kits by the hundreds.

Tools for Turning

There are hundreds of tools to choose from, but you can let your experience guide you along the way. Keep your initial tool purchases simple.

If you are setting up a dedicated turning area, you should have a lathe, a sharpening grinder, and a band saw. These are the basic tools needed to start. There should be adequate lighting and ventilation and a place to store some of your turning stock. Be advised that turning will produce a lot of wood shavings. (They provide great mulch for your garden.)

A beginner's turning set should include six high-speed steel tools:

- $3/8$" spindle gouge
- $3/4$" roughing gouge
- $1/2$" skew chisel
- $1/2$" round-nose scraper
- $1/4$" bowl gouge
- V-parting tool

Choose tools with handles that are at least 12" to 16" long in order to have better leverage and reduce vibration. To help maintain your turning tools, also consider investing in the following:

- A small, low-speed grinder equipped with a white aluminum oxide wheel, which will help you keep your tools sharp.
- A small diamond file to hone the sharpened edges.
- A set of inside/outside calipers to measure your work.

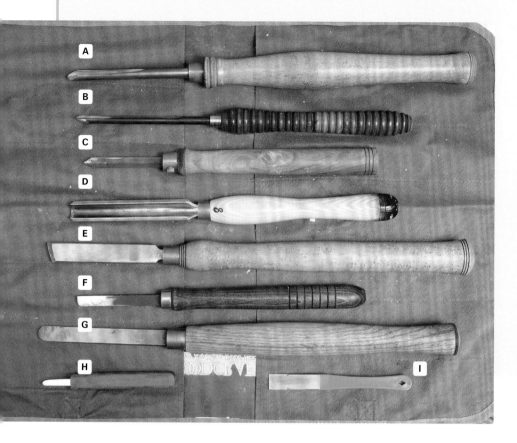

Having a low-speed grinder equipped with aluminum oxide wheels will help prevent overheating and taking the temper out of the cutting tools. There are commercial grinding and sharpening jigs that attach to the grinder to shape the proper angles on the various tools. After grinding the proper shape, use a small diamond mini hone to dress, or hone, the edge of the tool. Sharpening is a frequent task. Edges dull quickly and require constant sharpening trips to the grinder.

Proper sharpening of gouges and tools is the key to successful turning.

| TIP | **Check Your Woodpile** |

Wood that has found its way to the firewood pile will sometimes yield the most beautiful grain ever imagined. The most knurly, twisted log can yield a bowl that is an award-winner.

TOOL GLOSSARY

Roughing gouge: The most commonly used lathe tools are the gouges. Roughing gouges are used for roughing out square stock and reducing it to a cylindrical shape. They are also used for cutting coves or grooves on spindle turning. Gouges are normally sharpened with a 30- to 35-degree bevel. They have a square nose.

Skew chisel: The skew chisel is used in making beads, V cuts, and conical shapes. Skews have a bevel on one or both sides of the blade. The cutting edge has an angle of about 30 degrees across the face.

Bowl gouge: The bowl gouge resembles a spindle gouge except it is wider and relieves more wood in large areas. The tip is rounded.

Spindle gouge: The spindle gouge is used for detail work in spindle turning and for cutting hollows. The tool needs a long bevel sharpened to 30 to 45 degrees. The tip is rounded.

V-parting tool: The V-parting tool is used with calipers to establish sizing diameters for duplicating parts. It is used to make shoulders next to beads and to make tenons. The cut has flat sides and a flat bottom. The parting tool is sharpened at a 50-degree angle on each side. This tool makes a scraping cut.

Scrapers: Scrapers are used to smooth and refine already turned surfaces. They are used for both internal and external areas and excel for end grain hollowing. The bevel on the underside is ground to 40 degrees. The top of the scrapers is flat and they come in square-nose and round-nose versions. The square-nose chisel is usually used to give a smooth finish to convex surfaces, while the round-nose chisel is used on concave surfaces.

The scraper tools do not cut into or slice wood like a gouge does. They eliminate rough marks left by gouges and remove the high spots. You can tell when they are scraping well when fine, furlike shavings appear.

Learning to master the roughing gouge and remove lots of wood will give you a feel and confidence to proceed with the round-nose gouges.

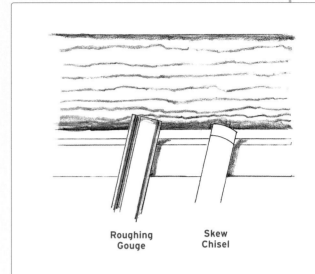

Roughing Gouge   Skew Chisel

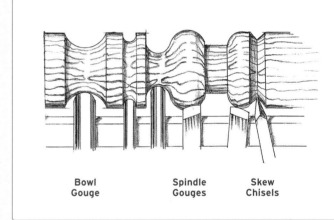

Bowl Gouge   Spindle Gouges   Skew Chisels

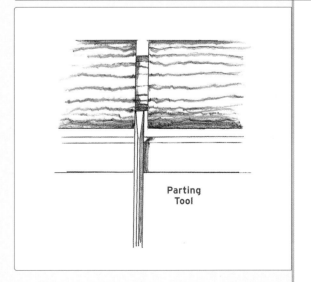

Parting Tool

CHOOSING A LATHE

There are many shapes and sizes of lathes available, and this choice can feel like deciding what style and kind of car you should purchase. (You can even buy used and new lathe models online or from classified ads.) Most new lathes offer electronic variable speeds and horsepower ranging from ½ to 3 hp. The small mini-style lathes offer a 12" swing, which means they can turn a piece with a maximum 12" diameter. They can turn spindles up to a length of 16". Some of these smaller lathes change speeds using the traditional belt-changing systems.

Be sure to research what is available while considering the type of turning work you plan to do. You can always do small work on a larger lathe, but a small lathe will not do larger work.

ABOVE Most of these types of lathes have variable speed controls. A large faceplate is shown attached to the lathe. A four-jaw chuck can also be attached to this type of lathe as well as a spur drive.

TOP, RIGHT Small faceplates are available and the wood blank is attached by screws.

BOTTOM, RIGHT The author's ½-hp lathe, which will turn 12" diameter bowls or 16" spindles

PARTS OF THE LATHE

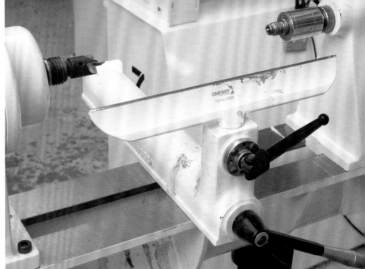

TOP, LEFT The head stock can accommodate a spur drive that is held in by its tapered shaft. A faceplate can also be screwed to the head stock after tapping out the spur drive.

BOTTOM, LEFT The tail stock holds a rotating center that supports the other end of the material being turned.

TOP, RIGHT The tool rest supports the cutting tools as they are presented to the turning wood rotating between centers. The tool rest can be rotated, raised or lowered, and moved forward and back on the ways. This lathe has variable speed control and a reversing capability.

BOTTOM, RIGHT A universal chuck attaches to the head stock. It has the capacity to hold a wide range of stock shapes and sizes.

The lathe that is pictured in this chapter is a "OneWay" product. It is one of ten lathes used in the Peters Valley Craft Center wood department classroom. Steven Antonucci, one of the founders of the Water Gap Wood Turners, was kind enough to do the turning demonstrations for this chapter. He teaches and demonstrates at many turning schools and seminars throughout the United States.

Turning a
WOOD PROJECT Spindle

When a square or rectangular piece of wood is cut on a lathe, it is classified as a spindle. The cutting tool cuts across the grain, which allows the turner to make a small object such as a pen blank or a larger piece such as a baluster or newel post. Most finials are turned in this manner and later carved by hand to achieve detail. Bottle stoppers, salt and pepper shakers, drawer pull knobs, baseball bats, and candle holders are all examples of objects made with spindle turning.

TOOLS

- roughing gouge
- spindle gouges
- rectangular turning blanks
- a lathe

When turning between centers, the wood is supported on one end by the tail stock that contains a live center. A live center is a bearing that rotates with the piece being turned, which reduces friction. The other end is centered and driven by the spur center on the head stock. The cutting tool cuts across the grain because the grain runs parallel to the lathe bed. Long cylindrical shapes and many profiles can be achieved. Different cutting tools and gouges are used to make coves, beads, tapers, and cylinders.

Care should be taken when applying the roughing gouge to spinning wood. Start with the gouge handle low and gradually lift the handle until the gouge starts cutting. The roughing gouge will come in contact with spinning wood at only the four corners. This will be a bumpy process until the corners start to be cut away. Continue with this process until you have formed a smooth cylinder. Now you can start using your spindle gouges to create coves and beads.

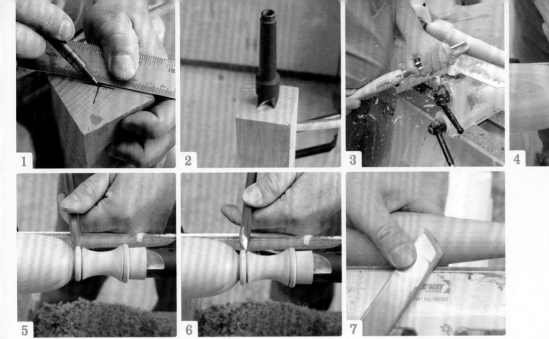

1. Find the center of the square stock by drawing straight lines from corner to corner on the ends of the stock. Where the lines intersect will be the center of the wood blank. Use a nail or awl to start a center hole.

2. Tap the spur center firmly into the starter hole using a mallet or piece of wood. Don't use a metal hammer because it will mushroom the end. Make sure the four spurs are driven into the blank, as they will spin the wood.

3. With the blank locked in between centers, move the tool rest parallel and close to the blank. Rotate the blank by hand to make sure it clears the tool rest. The tool rest should be centered on the axis of the blank. Lock everything in place. Put on a safety face shield for protection.

    Turn the blank by hand to make sure it clears the tool rest. Set the motor speed of the lathe on slow. Start using the roughing gouge to take down the square edges and start to create a cylinder. Continue shaping with the gouge from left to right. As the cylinder becomes smooth, increase the motor speed to make cleaner cuts.

4. Continue to establish the contours with a gouge, always cutting downhill and twisting the tool as you cut. This will allow you to cut away from the grain instead of into it.

5. Shape the bead with a spindle gouge. Relieve wood on each side of the bead with a parting tool or a skew point. Place the spindle gouge to the right of center with the tool angled to the right.

6. Cut down the right-hand side, moving the handle to the right, and roll the gouge clockwise. Repeat this for the opposite side of the bead. Remember, always cut downhill.

7. Another way of getting a graduated, smooth finish is to hold the skew chisel against the rotating spindle and apply light pressure with your hand.

    When presenting the tool to the wood, as seen in step 4, start with the gouge handle low and the other hand on top of the gouge that is resting on the tool rest. Present the cutting edge of the gouge slowly into the wood until it starts to cut. Slowly lift the handle until the cutting begins. Be careful not to catch the corner of the gouge into the wood, as this will cause a tear that could ruin the piece.

Turning a Bowl from
WOOD PROJECT Green Wood

You will never need any trips to the lumberyard when you work with green wood. It's all around you! A neighbor may be taking down a tree. Make friends with the local road department or the local tree service. They are often glad to get rid of logs without having to haul them away. Many species and varieties of wood are available where you live. Your biggest investment may be a chain saw.

This cherry log was cut a year ago and has been lying on the ground since then. Checking can be seen radiating from the pith.

Turning green wood is a low-impact woodworking style. There is hardly any dust, the curls are easy to sweep up, and green wood cuts easily into the desired shapes. If the wood is still wet, you will get a fine spray as you cut.

There are certain things you should look for when evaluating green logs for wood turning:

- Check for nails, screws, barbed wire, or other foreign objects embedded in the log. They can be detected when a dark or black stain is visible. A metal detector can give you valuable feedback. Do not try to cut around these obstacles. Go for a cleaner piece or section.

- Look for bug infestation and dry rot. If the tree has been down for a long time, look for checking (or cracking) on the end grain. Cut 4" off the end and see how deep the checks go.

TOOLS

- chain saw
- band saw
- round-nose scraper
- V-parting tool
- bowl gauge
- a universal chuck
- a lathe

Turning green wood is ideal for the beginner. Because the wood still contains a lot of moisture, it will be easier to cut. You will have a lot of extra wood to practice with before you finally get down to the shape of the bowl.

Select the log you want to work with and prepare it to make a blank. Begin with a chain saw to cut the log in half vertically. Make the cut off center to exclude most of the pith. Make sure the length is no longer the turning radius of your lathe. Lay the cut log flat on the band saw and cut off all four corners to remove excess wood. One side will still have bark on it. Chisel away the bark in the center to expose the wood. Eyeball the center on both sides so it can be positioned somewhat centered in the lathe. Lock it up and check for an even rotation.

1. Place the log on a cutting stand and cut several inches off the end to see how deep the splits go. Always wear hearing and eye protection.

2. If there are no checks inside, cut off a 14" blank.

3. Cut the log down the middle slightly to the right of the pith, or center. This will eliminate any pith appearing on the bowl blank.

1   2   3

(continued on page 144)

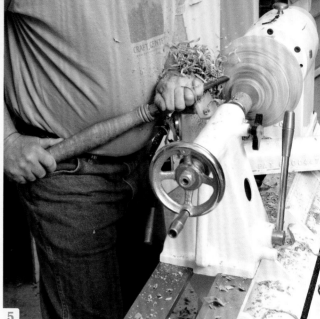

4. Trim the blank with a band saw to eliminate the bark and the corners. Place the blank between centers and lock down. This is called face grain turning.

5. Shape the outside of the bowl first with a bowl gouge. Push cuts from the bottom and center toward the outside and top of the bowl. Notice the wet curls coming off the bowl. The tool should rest against your hip for support. Use your left hand to hold the gouge down on the tool rest.

   Shaping the bowl is a visual thing. There are no set rules as to this shape, but enough wood should be left on the outside to allow for the inside to be shaped.

6. Cut a tenon at the base of the bowl with a V-parting tool so it can be gripped by the universal chuck. The tenon should be a ¼" deep and the

shoulder flat or 90 degrees to the horizontal. This will allow for a nice tight fit when gripped by the chuck.

7. Let the chips fall where they may! With the bowl grasped by the chuck, the inside of the bowl can now be turned. Angle the tool rest into the bowl opening to support the same bowl gouge that was used on the outside. Make the cuts from the rim to the inside of the bowl.

The green bowl on the left with a pair of finished cherry bowls by Steven Antonucci.

Leave the wall of the bowl 1" thick. Because the bowl is turned green, put it in a paper bag to allow it to slowly dry; otherwise it might dry too fast and crack. In three or four months the bowl will be stable enough to continue the finished turning. Never put a green bowl in a plastic bag for storing. It will rot and mildew because it cannot breathe.

After the green bowl has dried, it is time to place it back in the lathe for its final rebirth. Cutting will still be done with the bowl gouge. The cutting of the dry wood will be different than when the wood was green. Keep the gouge sharp. It should produce curls of wood rather than the wet spaghetti-like curls that came from the green blank. The inside walls should

be cut down to about ¼" thick and should conform to the outside shape of the bowl. Feel with your fingers to check for a consistent thickness of the bowl walls.

Use the round-nose scraper to smooth any high spots on the inside of the bowl. Many turners prefer to use the scraper technique rather than sandpaper. Sandpaper can be used for the outside of the bowl. Some turners prefer to use the wood curls to hold against the spinning surface to create a nice patina, while others will finish with special waxes. There are many, many ways to finish your turnings. Experimentation will be the best teacher.

The Final Finish
and Gallery

Finishing is the final step to present the hard work and effort that was done to create a well-designed and well-executed piece of wood-working. The first thing that admirers will do is touch and feel the piece. If it is smooth and soft feeling, it will encourage further inspection. The best-constructed piece of woodwork can lose its value if the finish is poorly applied.

The type of finish you choose will vary according to where and how a piece is used. A finish can improve the appearance of the wood by accentuating attractive grain patterns and adding luster to the surface. It is also useful as it can seal stain or dye, it can make the wood better able to withstand wear and tear, and it can make the wood more water resistant.

Outdoor furniture is usually painted to help seal the wood from moisture and ultraviolet rays. A walnut table in the living room needs a finish that will accentuate the beautiful grain as well as protect it from the high use it will receive. The stained oak kitchen table requires a finish that will emphasize the rich grain as well as seal the wood from moisture and the tough, constant use. Certain finishes can yield a highly polished or glossy luster while others will produce a satin surface. These effects can also be created by hand-polishing applied finishes with varying grits of sandpaper or applying final coats of wax.

Surface Preparation

Before you apply any finish, the surface has to be smooth and scratch free. Coarse sanding and saw marks should be eliminated when working with solid woods, as should the milling marks left by planers and jointers. Many types of sanding machines are available for working on the wood. Lumpy, bumpy surfaces might need a belt sander to aggressively reduce the high spots. You can then switch to an oscillating or orbital sanding machine to refine the surface. Some orbital sanders have a connection to

 Sandpaper Tips

Sandpaper is available in even finer grits up to #400, #600, and beyond. These fine-grit papers are used to sand between finishing coats. To get into fine or contoured areas, use flexible foam abrasive sheets. Felt or foam sanding blocks with sandpaper can be used instead of sanding machines. Grade #0000 fine steel wool is also used to get into contoured or tight areas. Do not use steel wool when using water-based finishes because the water will make any leftover steel particles rust and will leave tiny little brown spots.

attach a vacuum hose to capture the dust. There are two types sanding disks used for orbital sanders. Some are self-adhesive while others use a hook-and-loop system. Hook and loop (also known as Velcro) is a fine mesh that allows quick adhesion and removal from the sander. All of these machines can be outfitted with sandpapers in grits that range from #60 (coarse) to #220 (fine).

As you sand, you should move from coarse grit to fine. Whether by hand or machine, start with #80-grit paper. Make sure this grade of paper is eliminating the rough surface before you start to sand with a finer grade. Work your way up through the different grades of paper. It is advisable to use a lamp to shine across the grain as you sand. This will quickly illuminate any missed areas or imperfections. The final sanding should be done with #150-grit paper.

Applying a sanding sealer such as shellac or a water-based sealer will raise the grain. After the sealer dries, the surface will feel furry. Now you can lightly sand by hand with #220-grit paper. Always sand with the grain, as this will yield a smooth surface on which to apply your stain or finish.

Watch the Veneer!

When sanding solid wood edge banding attached to plywood, take care not to sand away the veneer on the plywood. Make sure the solid edge banding is glued firmly to the plywood to begin with. You can then plane and sand the solid wood to the same level as the plywood.

CARD SCRAPERS

Card scrapers are used to smooth out slight dents or irregular grain in wood. Scrapers act like a mini plane, slowly shaving minute curls of wood. If the scraper is not sharpened properly, you will produce dust, not curls.

Sharpening a card scraper takes some practice. To do this you need to use a fine mill file and a burnisher (a hardened steel rod).

1. Clamp the scraper horizontally in a vise. Lightly stroke with the mill file to make a flat square edge to the scraper blade.
2. Use a 1000-grit water or oil stone to hone the flat edge. Follow up with a 4000-grit stone.
3. Remove the scraper and hold it flat on a 1000-grit stone and hone each side to remove any burrs caused by filing. Place the scraper upright in the vise. (Sandwich the steel scraper with wood when it is in the vise to protect it.)
4. Hold the burnisher at 90 degrees to the blade and draw it across the edge. Use firm pressure and start to increase the angle with additional passes, but do not exceed a 10-degree angle. This will create a hook on the edge of the blade. This hook is what you will scrape with. The same process can be done to a curved scraper.

Sanding options:

A. Oscillating sander sands in a back-and-forth motion.

B. Mini belt sander sands using a rotating sandpaper belt.

C. Orbital sander sands in a circular motion.

D. Orbital sanding disks have hook-and-loop backing to apply to orbital sanders.

E. Card scrapers come in different shapes for matching contours.

F. Many grades of sandpaper

G. Foam abrasive pads fit into contours and irregular shapes.

H. Sanding blocks

I. Adhesive-backed sandpaper rolls stick to oscillating sander pads.

Hand-Applied Finishes

In this chapter we focus on hand-applied finishes. This type of finishing will produce high-end results that in most instances will be as good as spray finishes. The small shop has neither the room nor financial means for an expensive spray booth. There are many products available to create quality finishes. They can be brushed on, wiped on, or rubbed in.

Finishes can be either solvent- or water-based. (You can apply water-based finishes over dry solvent-based stains, but don't use a solvent-based finish over water-based finishes.) New water-based finishes are being developed to replace some solvent finishes. This makes for a healthier, less toxic environment in the woodshop, and they are more ecologically friendly. Fast-drying water-based stains can be used with acrylic top coats for durability. Old-fashioned milk paint, which offers a soft, pastel-type color finish, is back in vogue. Water-based milk paint can take solvent- or water-based top coats.

Oils such as Tung or Danish oil (A) can be liberally applied to the surface with a brush. You can also warm the oil in a double boiler for faster penetration. Allow the oil to sit for about 15 minutes and then wipe off the excess with a soft rag. Let the first coat dry for

12 hours, then apply a second unheated coat using a #600-grit wet/dry sandpaper to create a mixture of oil and sanding dust that will fill the pores of the wood and create a smooth surface. Wipe the surface clean with a lint-free rag and let dry for another 12 hours. Repeat this process several times until the grain has a luster that telegraphs through the surface.

Shellac (B) comes in two forms. Flakes of shellac can be dissolved with denatured alcohol. Ready-mixed shellac can be purchased at home centers and paint stores. For finishing, always use the dewaxed variety. This will not compromise the adhesion of oil- or water-based finishes. Shellac is fast-drying and is applied using a pad or brush.

Wipe-on poly finishes (C) are easy to use and produce a smooth surface, free of brushmarks. They come in satin and gloss varieties. Drying time is usually 4 to 6 hours. Sanding with #220-grit paper between coats produces a lustrous, protective surface.

Oil-based stains (D) are the most popular stains used because of the large range of colors available. They are easy to apply with a bristle or foam brush. The stain can be wiped off after 10 or 15 minutes with a clean soft cloth. Drying time is usually 12 hours. Water-based stains are also available. These stains dry fast but surface preparation is needed before applying stain. Wet the surface with distilled water and let dry. This will raise the grain, which then can be sanded with #220-grit paper. This will leave a smooth surface on which to apply the water-based stain.

Water-based finishes (E) are easy and safe to use. They dry fast and yield a tough surface. These finishes can be used on raw wood, shellac, water-based stains, and milk paint. The acrylic finish looks milky in the can and when first applied to the surface. When dry, the finish will be clear and hard.

Butcher block finish (F) is food-safe oil that can be applied to raw wood. The surface should be sanded smooth with #220-grit paper before applying this finish. This finish takes 12 hours to dry. Sand with #220-grit and reapply. It can be used on cutting boards, eating utensils, and salad bowls, or any other wood that comes in contact with food.

Paste wax (G) can be used over existing finishes to give a protective patina. It can be applied directly to wood with steel wool to rub the wax into the grain. This process will take several applications. Some specialty waxes come in different colors.

Milk paint (H) is not found in most paint or home centers but can be ordered through woodworking catalogs or the Internet. Milk paint comes as a powder. Many colors are available and they can be mixed with each other to produce the desired effect. The powder is mixed half and half with water. It takes a good amount of stirring to dissolve the powder but some small lumps will still remain. This slurry should be poured through a paint strainer into a separate container before using. Frequent stirring is needed to keep the solids from settling.

Correcting and Preventing Mistakes

No matter how good a craftsperson you are, mistakes always loom around the corner. As you start the finishing process you may find a split or check in the wood that you hadn't seen before you milled your lumber. Finding a glue spot when stain is applied to the surface is a common mistake. There are many ways to correct or prevent these types of errors.

GLUE SPOTS

Glue spots are a common problem. Care should be taken when gluing up your project. Glue squeeze out occurs when too much glue is applied to the joint. Do not use a damp cloth to wipe away the glue. This just washes the glue into the grain. This is a difficult mistake to fix because it's hard to see the glue smudge after it dries.

If the glue squeeze out is at an inside corner, use a drinking straw cut on an angle to scoop away the excess glue before it dries.

Another way to tame squeeze outs is to let the glue start to dry. Before it dries hard, use a chisel to scrape away the pliable excess. Use a card scraper to clean up the joint. The chisel and card scraper are the best tools for eliminating dried glue. Wiping wood with mineral spirits will help expose hidden glue spots before you begin to finish the project.

DENTS ON THE SURFACE

Slight dents that appear on the surface can be coaxed to raise themselves by steaming. Wipe distilled water across the wood to expand the wood fibers. Always use distilled water as it contains no minerals that could stain the wood. Place a dampened clean white cloth on top of the dent. Use a hot iron set at cotton temperature (high) and place over the cloth for 30 seconds. Keep checking the dent to see if it swells back close to the surface. You may have to repeat this process several times. Let the area dry and use sandpaper or a card scraper to feather, or blend, out the area.

To reduce the possibility of marring your project by mistake, use a moving blanket or carpet on the workbench.

REPLACING CHIPS AND BROKEN EDGES

Slivers of wood that break off can be reattached using cyanoacrylate glue. Use an activator spray made for this type of glue for an immediate bond. If there are any voids, place some white glue in the void and sand the area. The sawdust and glue will fill the crack. When the glue and sawdust dry, the crack should disappear. Sand off any residue.

Finishing the Laminated
WOOD PROJECT Wood Salad Tongs

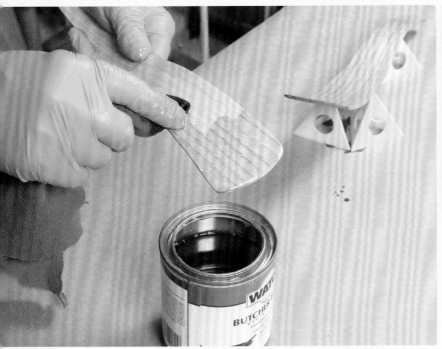

Laminated wood salad tongs; project on page 89.

TOOLS

- butcher block finish
- vinyl gloves
- #220-grit sandpaper
- soft cotton rags
- painter's points

1. Carefully sand with #220-grit sandpaper. Make sure to soften all the edges and any glue residue.

2. These tongs will be used to handle food, so apply a food-safe finish such as butcher block oil. Apply the first coat and put aside to dry for 24 hours. Then sand with #320-grit sandpaper and recoat with more finish. (Number 320-grit is very fine; it will not cut deeply into the surface but will allow good adhesion for the next coat of finish.)

   Apply a third coat of oil, repeating the above steps. Three applications of oil will help protect the tongs from their continued exposure to moisture. When the salad tongs start to get dull with use, an application of mineral oil is the best way to seal them from moisture.

Finishing the Veneered
WOOD PROJECT Flower Pendant

Flower pendant; project on page 97.

TOOLS

- satin wipe-on poly
- mineral spirits
- #220-, #300-, and #400-grit foam-backed sanding pads
- soft cotton rags

Special care should be taken when sanding the pendant. The veneer layers are very thin and can be sanded through quickly.

1. Start by using #220-grit foam-backed sanding pads. These pads are very flexible and will easily conform to the irregular shapes of the petals.

2. You can now switch to a finer grit such as #300 and continue the smoothing process. Be careful with the thin veneers. Use a soft rag, called a tack cloth, lightly moistened with mineral spirits to eliminate the sanding dust. You could also use a blast from the air hose if you have a compressor.

   Liberally apply wipe-on poly to the pendant with a soft cloth on the front face. Let this dry for 3 hours and then do the same to the back. After both sides have dried you can lightly sand with a #400-grit foam pad. Remember to use the tack cloth between each sanding. This process should be repeated three times. The last coat of poly should not be sanded.

Finishing the Shaker-style
WOOD PROJECT End Table

The Shaker-style end table shows a contrast in color and finish. The front of the drawer was painted while the drawer sides were left natural. Project on page 78.

The Shakers used simple ways of finishing their furniture, either a natural finish using oils or milk paint. The base of this table is painted with milk paint (see page 150).

TOOLS

- package of milk paint powder
- 2" foam brushes
- vinyl gloves
- oil-based stain
- mineral spirits
- #220- and #400-grit sandpaper
- poly acrylic finish
- oil finish

1. Apply water-based poly over milk paint as a seal coat. Blond shellac is another seal coat option. Some finishers prefer to leave the painted surface natural with no sealer applied.

2. Use nonslip pads to support the top while applying finish. This will allow the edges to be easily worked on during the finishing process.

3. Sand the top smooth with #220-grit sandpaper. Wipe the surface with a tack cloth and then apply an oil-based stain with a foam brush.

4. Let sit for 15 minutes, and then wipe the stain off with a soft cloth. Put aside to dry for 24 hours.

5. Apply three coats of oil finish. Each coat should dry for 24 hours. Sand with #400-grit sandpaper between each coat to give the surface some adhesion with the next coat. Remove the dust after each sanding. This process will yield a smooth, hard finish on the tabletop.

Finishing the Shadow
WOOD PROJECT Box Frame

The frame is now ready to hang on the wall or rest on a table. Project on page 62.

TOOLS

- shellac
- denatured alcohol
- mineral spirits
- wipe-on polyurethane
- #220- and #400-grit sandpaper
- cotton cloths

Mix and apply a 50/50 coat (equal amounts of shellac and denatured alcohol) of nonwaxed shellac to the walnut frame. Let the shellac coating dry for 45 minutes. It will act as a sanding sealer.

1. Sand the frame lightly with #220-grit sandpaper to eliminate any raised grain created by the shellac.

2. Moisten a cloth with mineral spirits to make a tack cloth and clean the dust made by the sanding.

3. Wipe on a coat of poly with a lint-free cloth. This application will dry in four hours and can be lightly sanded with #400-grit sandpaper. Use the tack cloth to reapply the finish. Repeat this process until the desired finish is achieved.

Presenting the
WOOD PROJECT Presentation Box

The finished presentation box.
Project on page 68.

2

3

4

5

TOOLS

- denatured alcohol
- mineral spirits
- shellac
- paste wax
- #100-, #150-, #220-, and #300-grit sandpaper
- cheesecloth
- cotton cloth
- ¼" fiberboard

The presentation box is ready for a shellacking! The highly figured walnut box should be sanded starting with #100-, then #150-, #220-, and finishing with #320-grit papers. This process will expose the beautifully figured grain both on the box and lid.

1. Mix and apply a 50/50 wax-free shellac and alcohol mix to the box using a padded ball made of wadded up cheese cloth wrapped with a cotton cloth.

2. Repeat this procedure four times, sanding with #400-grit sandpaper between each step. The grain will really start to pop!

3. Follow steps 1 and 2 on the top of the box.

4. Following the shellac applications, rub a paste wax in with fine steel wool. Use a soft clean cloth to polish the wax. This leaves a patina that exposes all that wonderful grain.

5. Make a bottom insert using some good fabric wrapped around a piece of fiberboard and taped on the back. The fit should be tight. This is the finishing touch.

Finishing the
Hanging Euro-style
WOOD PROJECT # Wall Cabinet

The finished wall cabinet, ready to hang on the wall. Project on page 72.

TOOLS

- pneumatic brad or pin nailer
- magnet
- green or blue tape
- cotton rags
- #0000 steel wool
- shellac
- denatured alcohol
- wipe-on poly
- #220- and #320-grit sandpaper
- yellow glue

This small wall cabinet will be stained first, then receive a protective top coat. Oil-based pigment stain penetrates plywood much more quickly than it does solid wood. To help eliminate this problem, a sanding sealer such as wax-free shellac will help to neutralize the surfaces and help to absorb the stain more consistently.

1. Apply shellac to the inside and outside of the cabinet. Sand and then add another coat of shellac. Sand again.

   Let the inside of the cabinet remain natural and stain the outside. Use tape to protect the inside as you apply stain to the outside. Wipe away the stain and put aside to dry for 24 hours.

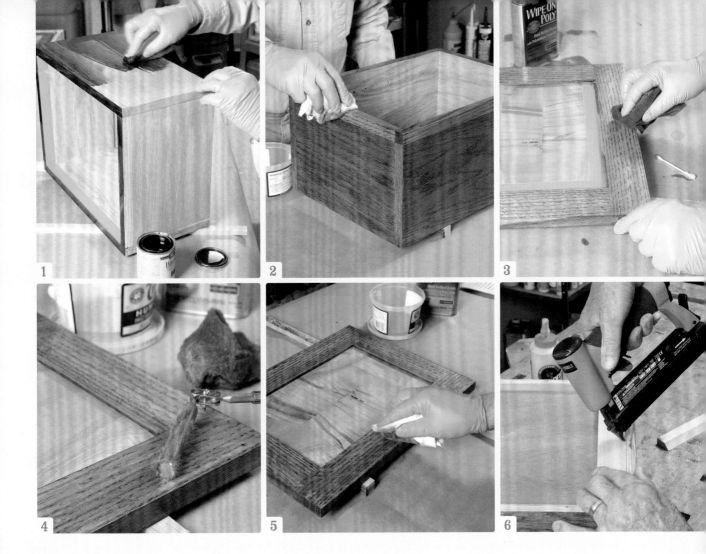

2. Apply three coats of wipe-on poly. Sand between each coat. You will not need poly on the inside.

3. Apply stain to the frame of the cabinet door and then wipe off. Use tape to protect the door panel from the stain. Finish the door panel before gluing the door so the panel can be completely sealed and finished before assembly. Apply wipe-on poly to the frame, using a cotton swab to reach the tight corners.

4. Rub down the first coat of poly with #0000 fine steel wool. Steel wool is easier to control in contoured or tight areas than sandpaper. This leaves a fine abrasion to the finish to help the next coat adhere to the surface. This is repeated for each of three coats. Capture steel wool residue with a magnet or a blast from the air hose.

5. Add the final coat of poly. Now the door is ready to hang on the cabinet.

6. Glue the back of the cabinet and brad-nail it to the rabbet in the back. Glue the French cleat and nail it to the back panel.

The Woodworker's
Gallery

The works displayed in this gallery are pieces from artisans who have been associated in one way or another with the Peters Valley Craft Center in Layton, New Jersey. Some pieces are made by teachers while others are made by students and assistants.

Carving Spotlight:

CARVED LAMP BASE

This lamp, which demonstrates how wood turning and carving can be elegantly combined, was made in three pieces. The leaf motif on the top was turned to give the flared shape, then carved to give the leaf detail. The body was turned and drilled to receive the cord for the lamp. It was then carved while still held on the lathe. The agate shapes were traced on the body and then relieved to match. The agates are glued in with epoxy. The base was turned and drilled, then all three were glued together. The walnut lamp was finished with wipe-on polyurethane.

This lamp by Jim Whitman is a good example of combining carving with wood turning.

Carving Spotlight:

LOW RELIEF CARVING

This Mucha-inspired carving was an experiment in low relief carving using mixed media and woodworking elements to complete this picture. The actual poster used for reference had much more detail. I simplified my drawing to emphasize the main figure. Detail sketches were made to work out some elements, such as how to have the hair drape over the frame. The frame also had to have a recess carved into it to accommodate the overlapping hair. Basswood was used to carve in. Two panels of ¾" wood had to be glued up to make the panel wide enough.

I had to establish the highest and lowest areas. I determined that the deepest cut was to be no more than ⅜". I then established what part of the figure was closest to the foreground. Because the figure leans over toward the viewer, the nose and chin were the areas to carve down from. The upper area of the hair was also on this same plane. The body part farthest away from the viewer (and thus the deepest cut) is the abdomen.

I taped my drawing to the wood at the top edge, which allowed carbon paper to be slipped under the drawing. Then I traced the drawing onto the wood. After removing the drawing, I used a pencil to darken any lost detail. Using gouges that matched the outline of the figure and a knife, I made ¼" deep stop cuts around the figure. Using a #5 gouge, I scooped out the background down to the stop cuts.

Lighter stop cuts were made in the interior body parts, such as the chin, arms, hands, and hairline. I then carved lightly into these new stop cuts. The edges of the hands, arms, and shoulders were rounded over. The hair that is in back of the face, arm, and bust were carved back slightly to give dimension. Subtle shaping and relieving were done, but care was taken not to carve too deeply. The highest and lowest areas of the craving are only about 5/16" apart. The background carving is only ⅜" deep.

This low relief carving was inspired by a poster by 1800s artist Alphonse Mucha. The piece combines carving, gesso, acrylic paint, gold leaf, and an oak frame carved to allow the hair to overlap the wood.

I used a V tool to create all the swirls in the hair. The back of the hair that overlaps the frame is cut away, leaving ¼" of thickness. The outline of the curls was cut out with a scroll saw. This shape was traced on the frame and carved out ¼" deep. The carving was lightly sanded, leaving some tool marks in the background. This tells the viewer that piece is carved, not molded. A light coat of gesso was then applied to seal the wood and form a smooth base for painting. A thin wash of acrylic paint was applied to the body, gold leaf was applied to the hair, and the body was outlined with a thin black marker.

The frame was then assembled and finished with wipe-on polyurethane. The carved panel was placed into it and fastened from the back.

A low relief carving insized in a slab of walnut by Jim Whitman. The depth of carving is ony ¹/₂" deep.

A 5½" square mahogany and tiger maple box by David VanHoff.

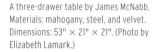

A three-drawer table by James McNabb. Materials: mahogany, steel, and velvet. Dimensions: 53" × 21" × 21". (Photo by Elizabeth Lamark.)

Spring 2005 desk by Jere Osgood. This is one of the many variations on his desks. It is loaded with techniques he has developed but more important is the design. It was meant to be an inviting place to sit, write, and develop new ideas. The design of this desk comes from the feeling for shape and form that he has developed over the years. (Photo by Bill Truslow.)

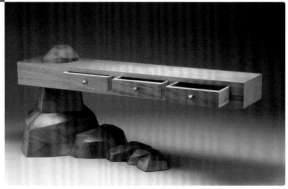

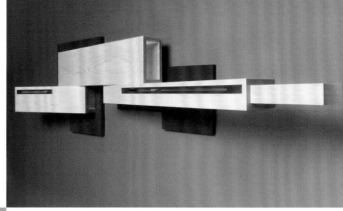

"Latitude." A wall sculpture by Jake Mendez. Materials: maple, bronze, and milk paint. Dimensions: 56" × 6" × 19". (Photo by Elizabeth Lamark.)

Jim Whitman used twelve species of wood to make the end grain top for this coffee table. The aprons are maple with grooved painted bars. The feet are walnut with maple plugs.

Another variation on an end grain table by Jim Whitman. Quarter-sawn red oak and walnut make up the rest of the end table.

An antique wood type lamp by Jim Whitman. The wood type surrounds the back and sides of this three-drawer lamp base. Materials: white oak, walnut, glass, and reproduction Hamilton drawer pulls. The drawers were made using hand-cut dovetails.

Hollow vessels turned by Steven Antonucci. Left: Curly Afzelia vessel. Center: Redwood burl. Right: Spalted maple.

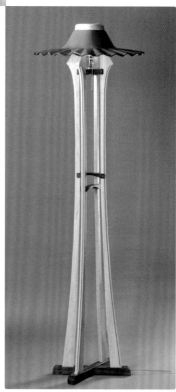

A floor lamp by Jim Whitman. An old enameled street light reflector was used for the shade of this lamp. The wood is ash and walnut.

This Prairie-style lamp was built by Jim Whitman from plans seen in a magazine fifteen years prior. The wood is cherry and ebony with bird's eye maple and anigre veneers. The leaded glasswork was made by his daughter, Bonnie Skillman.

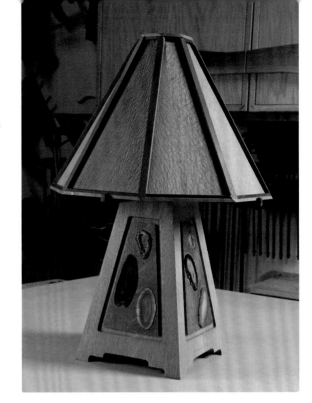

Arts and crafts-style lamp by Jim Whitman. The base of the lamp is quarter-sawn white oak with agate inlays. The shade uses rosewood and walnut ribs with lacewood veneer.

"Madam Butterfly" music stand by Jim Whitman. The bent lamination legs are made of walnut and maple. The wings are cherry and Italian plum. The center post is carved walnut.

Bent lamination table by James McNabb.
Dimensions: 37" × 24" × 21".
Materials: poplar, plywood, and acrylic.
(Photo by Elizabeth Lamark.)

Addison's Toy Box by Jim Whitman. Materials: walnut, oak, and poplar. The drawer handles are carved walnut. (Photo by David Hill.)

Presentation box by Jim Whitman. The box is flame walnut with maple corner keys. The top is book-matched maple. It has a padded insert on the bottom.

A chair by Jake Mendez titled "Night." Dimensions: 17" × 16" × 30". Materials: ebonized ash and micro-suede. (Photo by Elizabeth Lamark.)

An intricate turning challenge by Harvey Fein. Copper wire was woven into the platter for additional effect. It is turned using Jatoba wood from Africa.

"On the Rocks," a sculptural panel by Jim Whitman. The frame is cherry with maple corner keys. The inner panel is bird's eye maple supported with brass rods. The river rocks are set into the panel and glued with epoxy.

A pyramid jewelry box by Jim Whitman. Materials: stacked plywood, cherry top and drawer fronts, maple drawer pulls, and rosewood feet.

APPENDIX I:
Measurement Conversions

Lumber Dimensions

Nominal – U.S.	Actual – U.S. (in inches)	Metric (in mm)
1 × 2	¾ × 1½	19 × 38
1 × 3	¾ × 2½	19 × 64
1 × 4	¾ × 3½	19 × 89
1 × 5	¾ × 4½	19 × 114
1 × 6	¾ × 5½	19 × 140
1 × 7	¾ × 6¼	19 × 159
1 × 8	¾ × 7¼	19 × 184
1 × 10	¾ × 9¼	19 × 235
1 × 12	¾ × 11¼	19 × 286
1¼ × 4	1 × 3½	25 × 89
1¼ × 6	1 × 5½	25 × 140
1¼ × 8	1 × 7¼	25 × 184
1¼ × 10	1 × 9¼	25 × 235
1¼ × 12	1 × 11¼	25 × 286
1½ × 4	1¼ × 3½	32 × 89
1½ × 6	1¼ × 5½	32 × 140
1½ × 8	1¼ × 7¼	32 × 184
1½ × 10	1¼ × 9¼	32 × 235
1½ × 12	1¼ × 11¼	32 × 286
2 × 4	1½ × 3½	38 × 89
2 × 6	1½ × 5½	38 × 140
2 × 8	1½ × 7¼	38 × 184
2 × 10	1½ × 9¼	38 × 235
2 × 12	1½ × 11¼	38 × 286
3 × 6	2½ × 5½	64 × 140
4 × 4	3½ × 3½	89 × 89
4 × 6	3½ × 5½	89 × 140

Metric Coversions

To convert:	To:	Multiply by:
Inches	Millimeters	25.4
Inches	Centimeters	2.54
Feet	Meters	0.305
Yards	Meters	0.914
Square inches	Square centimeters	6.45
Square feet	Square meters	0.093
Square yards	Square meters	0.836
Ounces	Millimeters	30.0
Pints (U.S.)	Liters	0.473 (Imp. 0.568)
Quarts (U.S.)	Liters	0.946 (Imp. 1.136)
Gallons (U.S.)	Liters	3.785 (Imp. 4.546)
Ounces	Grams	28.4
Pounds	Kilograms	0.454
Millimeters	Inches	0.039
Centimeters	Inches	0.394
Meters	Feet	3.28
Meters	Yards	1.09
Square centimeters	Square inches	0.155
Square meters	Square feet	10.8
Square meters	Square yards	1.2
Millimeters	Ounces	0.033
Liters	Pints (U.S.)	2.114 (Imp. 1.76)
Liters	Quarts (U.S.)	1.057 (Imp. 0.88)
Liters	Gallons (U.S.)	0.264 (Imp. 0.22)
Grams	Ounces	0.035
Kilograms	Pounds	2.2

APPENDIX II:
Estimating Template

Project: _____

Symbol	Part	Qty	Rough Dimensions		Final Dimensions		Stock		Board Feet	Lumber Cost	Material Cost
			Width	Length	Width	Length	Solid	Ply			

Resources

There is a world of woodworking resources to explore. Here are a few places to get started.

Books and Magazines

Fine Woodworking Magazine
The Taunton Press,
www.finewoodworking.com

Editors of CPi. *Black & Decker The Complete Guide to Built-Ins*. Minneapolis, MN: Creative Publishing international, 2011.

Editors of CPi. *Black & Decker The Complete Guide to Outdoor Carpentry*. Minneapolis, MN: Creative Publishing international, 2009.

Editors of CPi. *Black & Decker Trim & Finish Carpentry*. Minneapolis, MN: Creative Publishing International, 2010.

Hoadley, R. Bruce. *Understanding Wood: A Craftsman's Guide to Wood Technology.* Newtown, CT: The Taunton Press, 1980.

Maloof, Sam and Jonathan Fairbanks. *Sam Maloof, Woodworker*. New York: Harper and Row Publishers, 1983.

Nakashima, Mira. *Nature Form & Spirit: The Life and Legacy of George Nakashima*. New York: Harry N. Abrams, 2003.

Pye, Chris. *Elements of Woodcarving*. East Essex: Guild of Master Craftsman Publications Ltd., 2001.

Online Resources

American Craft Council
www.craftcouncil.org

Arrowmont School of Arts and Crafts
www.arrowmont.org

The Furniture Society
www.furnituresociety.org

Peters Valley Craft Center
www.petersvalley.org

Wood Suppliers

Certainly Wood
13000 Rt. 78
East Aurora, NY 14052
(716) 655 - 0206
www.certainlywood.com

Downes & Reader Hardwood Co., Inc.
Box 634-8 Commercial Blvd.
Blakeslee, PA 18610
www.downesandreader.com

Hearne Hardwoods, Inc.
200 Whiteside Dr.
Oxford, PA 19363
(888) 814 - 0007
www.hearnehardwoods.com

Kuiken Brothers Co., Inc.
175 Rt. 23
Sussex, NJ 07461
(973) 875 - 0810
www.kuikenbrothers.com

Lowe's Home Improvement Stores
(800) 445 - 6937
www.lowes.com

Willard Brothers Lumber
300 Basin Rd.
Trenton, NJ 08619
(800) 329 - 6519
www.willardbrothers.net

Tools and Hardware

CMT USA, Inc.
Carbide-tipped tooling and blades
307-F Pomona Dr.
Greensboro, NC 27407
(800) 268 - 2487
www.cmtusa.com

Forrest Manufacturing Co., Inc.
Saw blades and sharpening
457 River Rd.
Clifton, NJ 07014
(800) 733 - 7111
www.forrestblades.com

Lee Valley Tools
P.O. Box 1780
Ogdensburg, NY 13669
(800) 871 - 8158
www.leevalley.com

Lie-Nielsen Toolworks Inc.
P.O. Box 9, Rt. 1
Warren, ME 04864
(800) 327 - 2520
www.lie-nielsen.com

**Packard Woodworks Inc.:
The Woodturner's Source**
P.O. Box 718
Tryon, NC 28782
www.packardwoodworks.com

Q.V.P. VAKuum Pressing Equipment
74 Apsley St.
Hudson, MA 01749
(800) 546 - 5848
www.qualityvak.com

Rockler Woodworking and Hardware
4365 Willow Dr.
Medina, MN 55340
(800) 279 - 4441
www.rockler.com

Wood Carvers Supply, Inc.
P.O. Box 7500
Englewood, FL 34295
(800) 284 - 6229
www.woodcarverssupply.com

Woodcraft
P.O. Box 1686
Parkersburg, WV 26120
(800) 225 - 1153
www.woodcraft.com

Glossary

Air dried: Lumber that is allowed to dry slowly with normal air temperatures so it is protected from the elements. This type of slow drying is favored by some woodworkers, but the drying time is much longer than that of kiln drying.

Band saw: A saw blade that rotates on two or three wheels driven by a motor. The saw cuts wood that is placed on a table in front of the blade. The saw is designed to cut arcs and shapes.

Bench room: An area dedicated to hand work that is separated from noisy, dusty areas created by machines.

Biscuit joint: Slots that are cut into mating pieces of wood to create a butt joint. Biscuits are glued and inserted into the slots and then clamped together to create a strong butt joint.

Burnisher: A hardened steel rod that is used to create a burr on the edge of a card scraper. It is drawn over the edge of the steel scraper at a 10-degree angle.

Card scrapers: Flat pieces of steel with edges that have been filed flat, then honed. A burnisher is used to roll the edge of the card to create a burr that is then used to scrape and smooth wood surfaces.

Chamfer: An angle cut on the edge of wood using a plane, chisel, or sandpaper to enhance or soften the edge.

Cutting list: A detailed list of the sizes and species of every piece of wood needed to build a project.

Dust collector: A vacuum machine that is attached to a power tool to collect the wood chips and dust it creates.

Grain: The direction the wood grew (grain runs lengthwise along the original tree). Working with the grain prevents tear out while hand planing or putting wood through a jointer or planer.

Jointer: A machine that is used to plane the surface of a board smooth and square on one side.

Kerf: The width of a cut made by a saw blade.

Kiln dried: Lumber that is cut while green (or wet) and then put into a drying structure that extracts moisture through heat and air circulation. The ideal is to reduce the moisture content of the wood to about 6 to 8 percent.

Lamination: Thin strips of wood that are glued together and clamped onto a form to create a shape.

Marking gauge: A device used to transfer a measurement by scribing a mark on wood. It is adjustable to any size and is used for marking mortise and tennon and many other joints.

Miter joint: Two pieces of wood cut at 45-degree angles that are joined together to create a 90-degree corner. This joint is used to make frames, boxes, and cabinets.

Planer: A machine that planes (levels) both sides of a board smooth and parallel.

Router: A high-speed electric motor to which router bits can be attached to cut various shapes on the edges or the interior of wood panels.

Router bit: A cutting device that is attached to the router using a collet. Router bits come in hundreds of shapes and sizes and are made of high-speed steel or carbide cutters.

Router table: A table that has the router attached underneath with the router bit above the table. Wood is passed over the router bit.

Sharpening station: An area dedicated to sharpening chisels, plane blades, and knives.

Sheet goods: Manmade lumber such as plywood, MDF, Masonite, particle board, or any other 4' × 8' type of wood.

Standing drill press: The drill motor is attached to a column that is attached to a base. The height of the drill press table is adjustable on the column to allow different sizes and heights of wood to be drilled.

Stickers: Pieces of wood that are evenly placed between boards to enable air circulation during the air or kiln drying process.

Studio: An area for doing woodworking such as a basement, garage, out building, or a covered, protected outdoor area.

Table saw: The most common power tool in many shops, typically 10' in length. The wood rides over the saw guided by a fence or miter gauge. Most table saws have a tilting blade that allows cuts to be made between 90 and 45 degrees.

Task lighting: A dedicated light source to directly light the area in which you are working.

Tear out: A jagged or torn area in wood.

Template: A form shaped to allow a router with a guide bushing or a bearing guide to route the shape into a piece of wood.

Vacuum forming: A lamination technique in which glued parts can be clamped by inserting them into a vinyl plastic bag and removing the air with a vacuum pump after the bag is sealed. This will compress the bag to 15 PSI and effectively clamp the piece until the glue is set.

Veneer: Wood that is cut or sliced thin from exotic wood or prized logs. The veneer is then glued to secondary wood to create panels or formed into shapes.

Work bench: A table or bench to secure wood while it is addressed with hand or power tools.

Work flow: The smooth transition of steps in the process of preparing wood parts for assembly and finishing.

About
the Author

Photo by Bruce Byers and students at 2011 Peters Valley photography class.

Jim Whitman has been working with wood for more than forty years. He started woodworking as a hobby while directing his graphic design studio in Clifton, New Jersey. In 1973, Jim and his family moved to a farm in rural Lafayette, New Jersey, where he built a barn to house his wood shop. During this time he was introduced to the Peters Valley Craft Education Center in nearby Layton, New Jersey, where he was inspired by many great teachers. He studied with some of woodworking's eminent personalities including Tage Frid, Sam Maloof, Jere Osgood, Mack Headley, and Toshio Odote. Jim was so passionate about the mission of teaching crafts that he served on the Peters Valley Board of Directors for twenty years. In 2001, Jim retired from his graphics business and the Peters Valley Board to continue with his ever-increasing woodworking commissions, as well as teaching and consulting. Jim says, "I am so lucky to be able to work at what I love."

About
the Photographer

Randy O'Rourke, based in Kent, Connecticut, has photographed more than sixty books, many pertaining to woodworking, home construction, and home design. His photographs have also appeared in numerous national and regional publications and websites. His work can be viewed at rorphotos.com. In his spare time he enjoys hiking, traveling, and photographing sporting events.

Acknowledgments

I will never stop thanking my wife, Joanne, for her help in making me understand Microsoft Word, and her patience while I spent so much time on the computer and in the studio.

I must also remember my dear friend Ed Crowe. He was my mentor in the early 1980s. Ed was a woodshop teacher at a local vocational school, and in the evenings we would talk and make furniture in his basement workshop. I wish he were around today to read this book.

I would also like to thank the following people:

Kristin Müller, the director of Peters Valley Craft Center, who was kind enough to introduce me to Quarry Books and encouraged me to write this book.

Randy O'Rourke, the patient and creative photographer who traveled from Connecticut many times to shoot almost 400 photos used in this book. Neither sleet nor snow kept him from showing up for the photo sessions!

Steven Antonucci, who helped me with the wood turning chapter and was the model for these shots.

The many teachers, staff, and board members at Peters Valley Craft Center who have helped me in the past 30 years to achieve the success I have today.

Rochelle Bourgault, an acquisitions editor at Quarry Books. Her kind but firm guidance kept me on the right track. Also thanks to the wonderful team of designers and editors at Quarry, including Tiffany Hill, my exceptional project manager.

The artists that shared their work for this book: Jere Osgood, Harvey Fein, James McNabb, Jake Mendez, and Steven Antonucci.

To all my friends and associates who have helped and encouraged me throughout my career.

Index